D0753221

LANG LANG
PLAYING WITH FLYING KEYS

LANG LANG

PLAYING WITH FLYING KEYS

{ BY **LANG LANG**
WITH **Michael French**
introduction by
Daniel Barenboim }

DELACORTE PRESS

Published by Delacorte Press
an imprint of Random House Children's Books
a division of Random House, Inc.
New York

Text copyright © 2008 by Lang Lang
Map illustration copyright © 2008 by Rick Britton
Some material based on interviews with David Ritz, as well as Celina Spiegel and Beverly Horowitz.

Visit us on the Web! www.randomhouse.com/kids

Educators and librarians, for a variety of teaching tools, visit us at www.randomhouse.com/teachers

Library of Congress Cataloging-in-Publication Data is available upon request.
ISBN: 978-0-385-73578-0 (trade)—ISBN: 978-0-385-90564-0 (lib. bdg.)

The text of this book is set in 11.5-point Usherwood Medium.

Book design by Angela Carlino

Printed in the United States of America

10 9 8 7 6 5 4 3 2 1

First Edition

For my mother and father

陈阳 陈阳

LANG LANG
PLAYING WITH FLYING KEYS

CONTENTS

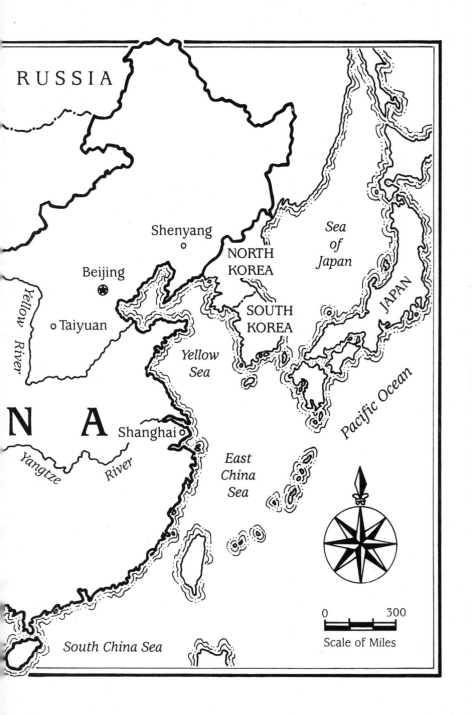

RUSSIA

Shenyang
○

NORTH
KOREA

Sea
of
Japan

Beijing
✪

JAPAN

Taiyuan
○

SOUTH
KOREA

Yellow
River

Yellow
Sea

N A

Shanghai ○

Pacific Ocean

Yangtze
River

East
China
Sea

South China Sea

0   300

Scale of Miles

LANG LANG'S JOURNEY

1982
Lang Lang is born in Shenyang, China.

1987 (age 5)
Lang Lang wins his first competition, in Shenyang, playing his first-ever recital.

1991
Lang Lang and his father move to Beijing.

1994
Lang Lang wins his first international award, in Germany.

1997
Lang Lang arrives in Philadelphia to study at the Curtis Institute of Music.

1999
Lang Lang is propelled onto the world stage when he replaces André Watts in a last-minute substitution with the Chicago Symphony Orchestra at the Ravinia Festival.

2001 (April)
Carnegie Hall debut. Then back to Beijing for the first time after coming to America. Plays at the Great Hall of the People with the Philadelphia Orchestra.

2001
Teen People magazine lists Lang Lang as one of the Top 20 Teens Who Will Change the World.

2003

Lang Lang featured in the "Best of *People*" issue for 2003.

2006

Plays opening of the World Cup concert (FIFA), Munich.

2006

Lang Lang plays at the White House.

2007

Lang Lang appears on a Golden Globe–winning soundtrack as featured soloist for *The Painted Veil.*

2007

Lang Lang plays in Tiananmen Square as part of a one-year countdown to the 2008 Beijing Olympics.

2007

Royal variety show for Queen Elizabeth II of England.

2007

Plays at the Nobel Prize Concert, Stockholm.

2007

Nominated for his first Grammy, for Best Classical Instrumentalist.

2008

Lang Lang plays at the 50th Annual Grammy Awards.

INTRODUCTION

Dear Children of the World,

How wonderful that you are going to read about the life of someone who most likely was very much like each and every one of you and has had the great luck to discover that he has a talent for music—as I am sure many of you have. Music is not only for some people; music is for everybody, anywhere in the world, of any age. Reading about Lang Lang will make you curious about what made him want to be a musician. Being a musician is important, and it is very serious, but it is also a lot of fun.

The hours that are needed to train are not always fun, as I remember already thinking at your age, but as with everything else in life, if you practice intelligently and with discipline, you will be free and able to enjoy yourself when you perform. For those of you who will eventually choose to do something else in life, I hope that this book will awaken in you the curiosity to find out how much pleasure and, yes, fun, you can derive from listening to music. One of the most wonderful things about music is that it is imagined and played at the same time.

Lang Lang, like all real musicians, has remained a child in the sense that he never ceases to wonder at the magic of music. If he has been able to transmit but a small part of that wonder to you, this book has more than succeeded.

Your music-loving friend,
Daniel Barenboim

PROLOGUE

I was only nine years old, a third-grade student from the city of Shenyang, China, when I knew my life was going to change. I tightly clutched my mother's hand, waiting at the Shenyang station for the train to take us to Beijing, my new home. My father would be waiting for me. For the previous forty-eight hours my body had been wracked by a high fever—every bone in my body ached—and in my nightmares monsters were chasing me. When the fever finally broke, my mother pronounced me fit enough to travel and helped me pack my suitcases.

I had never been to Beijing, but I knew my life would soon be very different, harder, more challenging. I was already a gifted young pianist, but my father insisted I move to Beijing to advance my musical skills. Part of me was eager to go; another part was incredibly sad. I would miss my friends, grandparents, and teachers in Shenyang. Most of all I would miss my mother. Still holding my hand, my mother, Xiulan, looked down at me with her big brown eyes and beautiful smile. I was trying to appear brave, but she had always been able to read my mind. "Do not feel lonely or afraid, Lang Lang," she told me. "You are a very special boy. Your music will always keep you company."

In Shenyang, I had been playing the piano since before I was two, and many in my city considered me a prodigy. I had entered my first piano competition at age five. Newspapers had written stories about me and published my photo. My father had long believed I was destined for greatness, and nothing would dissuade him. But nothing would be easy either. In China in 1991, a nine-year-old pianist had little hope for a career without attending the Beijing Conservatory and learning from the country's most accomplished teachers. This was my father's dream for me, and it had become mine as well.

Admission to the conservatory was extremely competitive. Everyone had to play his or her best work for the judges. There were also written exams. I would be competing against three thousand boys and girls my age from all over China. Only fifteen in my grade would be chosen for the conservatory, and to win a financial scholarship, a necessity for my family, I would have to be in the top eight.

The odds were against me. Since my father had quit his job to be with me, my family was poor and lacked influence in the world of music. My piano teacher since I was four, a woman named Professor Zhu, did not have the power of teachers from bigger cities. To those at the conservatory, whose authority and power would determine my future, I was practically invisible. But my father, a clever man, had anticipated all this. To make up for our disadvantages, he had ordered me to practice with incredible discipline since I was three years old. He knew that one day I would be competing against the best and brightest in a country of more than a billion people. I had only my talent to fall back on. I had to be prepared.

Now the moment of truth was near. Was I prepared enough for the conservatory judges? I knew my father would not tolerate failure. As the train pulled up on that gray, overcast morning and my mother and I waited for the conductor's signal to board, my blood rushed through my ears. Could I really succeed in Beijing? What if I disappointed my father? My mother reached over with her handkerchief to dab my tears.

"Your father will meet us at the train station. He has an apartment already picked out. And your piano will be waiting for you as well."

"But I want you to live with us, Mother." I couldn't stop crying.

"Lang Lang, I don't want to be separated from you either. But I need to stay at my job in Shenyang. I am our family's only breadwinner for now. Your father is sacrificing everything to get you into the conservatory. He must find you a new teacher in Beijing. There is much work to be done before the entrance exam."

There was no arguing with my mother. Her mind was made up, even if her heart was divided. I saw a tear in her eye and I wanted to wipe it away. She was to accompany me to Beijing, stay for a day or two until I was comfortable, and then return to Shenyang, where she worked as a telephone operator for China Science Institute, Shenyang quarter. I would miss her cooking, her stories, and her tenderness. My father was my motivator and disciplinarian, but my mother was my emotional anchor. I wondered how I could survive in a strange city of ten million people without her.

"Time to go," she said softly, pulling me along. "A great adventure awaits you. I know it in my heart, Lang Lang." They named me Lang Lang. In Chinese, my given name, *Lǎng,* means "brightness and sunshine," and my family name, *Láng,* means "educated gentleman." Thanks to my parents for having given me such a wonderful name, I now had to live up to their expectations.

I resisted for a moment, gazing back on the city of my birth. Shenyang was hardly a small city—it was the industrial capital of northeast China, with eight million people—but to a nine-year-old boy who knew only his neighborhood and his school, it was small indeed. I was flooded with memories and suddenly struck by what an incredible adventure my life had already been. Being a prodigy is a gift from the universe, a blessing bestowed on only a handful of people, my father had told me more than once. With that blessing come untold sacrifice and endless work, he added, along with the certain prospect of weathering many storms. How true that would prove to be.

PART ONE
THE CHINA YEARS

SHENYANG, 1982–1991

{ 1 }

I have many early childhood memories. Like strands in a tapestry, they weave a mixed impression—joy, hardship, hope, sadness, struggle, and success. Some strands stand out in vivid detail.

When I was two years old, a simple barracks apartment on the Shenyang air force base was our home. My father, a thin man of average height, was the silent type. In fact, he was stern and I have no memory of him smiling. He played professionally in the air force orchestra. We had very few luxuries, but they included an upright piano purchased by my parents when my father grew convinced I had a special gift for music. My mother later told me I could read musical notes before I learned the alphabet, and with my large hands and long fingers, I loved gliding my fingertips on the keys. Of course, I couldn't touch the pedals. In fact, I could only touch the keys by placing pillows on my piano bench. But my father said I was creating music, that I knew intuitively when the notes harmonized. Most important to me, I was filling my ear with beautiful sounds that in turn filled my imagination with incredible stories I made up as I played for hours at a time.

In the air force orchestra my father played the erhu—a popular folk instrument with two strings, a cross between a violin and a small bass—but he told my mother from the beginning that I should be taught the piano.

"The piano is the most beloved instrument in the world," he declared, and she agreed. My father, whose name is Lang Guoren, was my first teacher.

Zhou Xiulan also loved music. My mother had grown up listening to Peking Opera on the radio with her parents, and when she was a teenager, she developed a lyrical voice. She dreamed of singing in a concert. But the Cultural Revolution started in the 1960s. My parents' families were either property owners or intellectuals, and middle-class. My parents and their families moved from their homes in the city to distant rice farms, where they worked long hours. My parents lived in the countryside for five years. They did not know each other at that time.

When he was twenty-five years old, before being married to my mother, my father applied for admission to the Shenyang Conservatory of Music. Now back home, he was determined to forge a career for himself. His talent and dedication to the erhu were extraordinary, and among all the applicants that year he placed first on two entrance exams. But at the last moment, on a trumped-up technicality, he was denied admission.

I don't think his soul ever quite healed. I didn't understand any of this until I was older, but almost from the beginning, I felt his frustration and his high expectations for me.

"Practice, Lang Lang. Practice day and night. Do not dream of anything but being the best pianist you can be," he would say to me over and over.

My mother told him he was too strict, and sometimes he was, but his will almost always prevailed. "Don't pamper our son," he declared if he caught my mother reading me a story with my head against her shoulder. "He should be playing the piano, not listening to silly tales. He has a gift, but it means nothing without hard work. You're only spoiling him."

"He's just a little boy," she countered. "All boys need time to play and dream."

"He has his dream. Now go, Lang Lang, and play your lessons until it is time for supper."

I dreamed often the dream my father had for me, to become a great pianist. While I sometimes watched cartoons on a neighbor's television, played with other children on the air force base, and created my own fantasies around the stories my mother read to me, most of my time was occupied by the piano. I knew of other children in Shenyang who practiced long hours. They too dreamed of one day being admitted to the Central Conservatory of Music in Beijing. I had to play longer and better than my competitors. My father and I would have it no other way.

By the time I started school at age seven, Lang Guoren had fashioned an unyielding schedule for me:

5:45 a.m.: Get up and practice piano for an hour.
7:00 a.m.: Go to school.
Noon: Come home for a fifteen-minute lunch, then
forty-five minutes of piano.
After school: Two hours of practice before dinner
and a chance to watch some cartoon shows.
After dinner: Two more hours of practice, then
homework.

When I finished my homework and crawled into bed, it was late at night.

On occasion, when my father wasn't around, I would take a break from the piano and hang around my mother, helping her in the kitchen or listening to her wonderful stories. I knew how much she loved me by the way she doted on my smile and never tired of my endless questions.

I wanted to know everything about my mother's and father's families and how my parents had met and fallen in love. At first her father had not approved of Lang

Guoren because he had failed to win admission to the conservatory and he had no job prospects. But my father was persistent in all things, and when he was selected for the air force orchestra, my grandfather finally accepted his daughter's stubborn young suitor into the family.

My parents were married in April 1980, and a little more than two years later, on June 14, 1982, I came into this world by the skin of my teeth. My mother told me that the umbilical cord was wrapped so tightly around my neck that my face was green. The doctor had to work quickly.

"You mean I almost died," I answered, terrified by the thought, whenever she told this story.

"No, my child. You didn't die because you had work to do. You had music to bring into the world."

I would be my parents' first and only child, because in order to preserve its resources for a swelling population, the government began a one-child-per-family policy only in the city. This meant both my parents lavished an incredible amount of attention on me. While my mother's natural inclination was to nurture and indulge me, my father expected near perfection from his piano prodigy. After I turned four, every night he asked how many hours I had practiced that day. If my answer didn't please him, I would abandon whatever I was doing and go back to the piano. It was as if he thought a clock alone could determine my future. Because of the one-child policy, many children born in the 1980s were pushed and pressured by their parents. My experience of being pressed to the limit by my father was not the exception. Parents who had not achieved their own dreams put all their unrealized hopes onto their one and only child. This was especially true for future musicians, but it applied in the areas of sports and science as well.

What he didn't understand, and I was too young to explain, was the relationship between watching television or having my mother read to me and becoming a great pianist.

When I was around three, I remember watching an episode of *Tom and Jerry,* the American cartoon, where Tom the cat was a concert pianist. A cat in a tux was playing classical music! I convulsed with laughter. Inside the piano was Jerry, the little mouse, napping on the strings and felt. Wakened by Tom's playing, Jerry, annoyed, gave the cat a taunting wave, as if to distract him. Eager to keep playing, Tom ignored his archenemy. Jerry mischievously jumped out of the piano and onto the keyboard. Tom played faster. As the music sped up, so did the action. Tom caught his finger in a mousetrap set by Jerry. Furious, Tom threw Jerry under the piano bench. Jerry climbed back up and began hitting the keys to a jazz beat in the middle of Tom's classical piece. Cat and mouse fought furiously. The music and the fight were perfectly in sync. In the end, the more resourceful mouse wore out Tom. Jerry, now wearing a small tux, bowed to the applauding audience. I clapped too!

I later learned that the piece Tom played was the Hungarian Rhapsody no. 2 by Franz Liszt. At that age I had no idea what a composer or composition was, but I understood how much fun playing a piano could be. My imagination allowed me to be Tom one minute, Jerry the next. I wanted my fingers to fly over the keys just like Tom's! I imagined myself playing right next to them. I wanted to see how fast I could chase Tom and how quickly I could catch Jerry. I would see myself jumping and falling and then getting up and doing it all over again, even as my hands grew tired and my fingers ached from playing.

I understood at a very early age that not only was making music great fun, but it conveyed a secret language. It told me secret stories, and they were mine alone to hold in my imagination, like a pearl in an oyster.

There was another cartoon character that played an even greater role in stimulating my imagination and my growth as a pianist. His name was Monkey King. Monkey King was my hero. He stayed at my side when I played and practiced, when I went to bed, when I eventually got into disagreements with my father, or whenever I faced difficult times. I loved him not just because he was an adorable monkey who had a good heart and helped people in trouble, but because his job, in Chinese mythology from as far back as the Tang Dynasty, was to spread truth through the world. Music was my truth to spread, and Monkey King helped me with my mission.

Monkey King was also immortal. Because he had rebelled against the gods long ago, for punishment he was buried under a mountain for five hundred years. Only when he agreed to protect a certain monk on a pilgrimage to bring a holy Buddhist text through India to China did the gods agree to free him. Monkey King took seriously his assignment of protecting the monk, but he also liked to play pranks. I loved him because he was clever and because you could never catch him. He changed his shape at will. He could turn into a fish, a flea, a turnip, or a tree. Monkey King took on a million different shapes that suggested a million different stories—just like the music I played.

When he wasn't being mischievous, he was a hero. He protected children. He defeated anyone who tried to hurt him or the monk. He was on a journey to bring joy to the world. I loved him. Monkey King's power was unlimited because his imagination, like his heart, had no boundaries.

{2}

Around my fourth birthday, as my father listened to me practice, he had a revelation. Or perhaps he had known all along this moment would come.

"Lang Lang," he said, "I can no longer be your teacher."

"Why?" I asked, turning from the piano. I had come to depend on my father to guide me in what and how to play and to correct me when I made mistakes. Whatever he had asked of me, even things I didn't like, such as learning scales and tackling exercise books, I did without arguing.

"I have taught you everything I know. It's time we find

you a professional teacher. The very best in Shenyang. Number one."

The next day we went to an apartment on the grounds of the Shenyang Conservatory of Music and were greeted at the door by a small, delicate woman with clear, wise eyes. Her name was Zhu Yafen. I responded to my new music teacher as my father had instructed, with a deep bow.

I did my best to smile at her, but inside I was trembling. Monkey King was with me, and I also wore a green military uniform with two toy pistols tucked under my belt. I was nervous because my father was nervous. He had warned me that to gain admission to the Shenyang Conservatory, I needed lessons from the very best local teacher. I could not make a single mistake when I played for her. If she rejected me, he said, my career would be over before it started.

Professor Zhu smiled at my attire. "It is so nice to meet you, Lang Lang. Welcome to my home and studio. You might be more comfortable if I take these while you play," she suggested, pointing to my pistols. Her voice was as golden as honey.

I felt immediately at ease and safe with Professor Zhu. I didn't need my pistols. I asked, "Would you like to hear what I can play?"

I marched directly to her piano, placed two pillows on the bench so I could reach the keyboard, and began something from C. L. Hanon's *Virtuoso Pianist in 60 Exercises*. It was easy for me because I had practiced everything in the Hanon book so often, and because I imagined that Monkey King was beside me, smiling encouragement as my fingers swept over the keys.

"Will you accept him as a student?" my father asked almost as soon as I had finished.

"Yes, I will. Lang Lang plays with great spirit and energy. He enjoys the piano like a child enjoys a new toy."

"The piano is not a toy for my son. How talented do you think Lang Lang is?"

"Quite talented."

"He must be the number one pianist in all of China. And then all the world. Is that possible?"

Not once did my father smile. He was all business, focused totally on my future. He meant to sound purposeful, but he came across as boastful. My glance darted nervously to Professor Zhu. I was afraid that my father's attitude would change her mind about accepting me.

"At Lang Lang's age, I prefer to be patient," she replied. "He will show me what he can accomplish when he is ready."

"Do not be easy on the boy. Push him. Challenge him. There's nothing he can't do."

"Lang Guoren, your son has an astute ear, his hands are large and his fingers long and graceful, and he has an instinct for rhythm. But as critical as those gifts are, equally important, maybe more important, is his spirit. His spirit understands the greatness of the music he seeks to play. If we push him too much, his spirit could begin to question why he should play at all. I do not want to take that risk. If you do, you risk losing everything."

"Professor Zhu, you do not understand my son. He has another kind of spirit—the spirit to compete. If you make him, Lang Lang will practice harder. He will practice longer."

Professor Zhu was diplomatic but stubborn in her own way. I felt she cared about me in the same manner as my mother. "Children require recreation," she said. "They require rest and play, sunlight and nourishment. You can't rush their growth."

"Lang Lang is different from your other students. He wants to be the best. If you are too easy on him, you will hurt him."

I squirmed on the piano bench. Why did my father keep arguing? He never seemed to know when to stop after making his points. Professor Zhu responded by placing her hand on my shoulder. Years later she would tell me that as much as she disagreed with my father's approach, she understood where his anxiety and dreams for me came from. Her family too had been accused of "middle-class decadence" and relocated to a rice farm during the Cultural Revolution. Professor Zhu had to abandon her dream of becoming a concert pianist.

Twice a week I began taking lessons at Professor Zhu's studio, and right away I noticed the difference between her and my father's teaching style. First, she didn't mind if I brought along a toy. I had given up my pistols, but my favorite toys were Transformers, and through saving money here and there, I had collected quite a few. As with

Monkey King, I viewed my Transformers as my protectors. Second, when I arrived at the studio, Professor Zhu asked if I needed to use the bathroom, or if I was thirsty or hungry. She always told me to relax, a word that was not in my father's vocabulary.

"Yes, child, just relax," she repeated whenever I looked up at her to see how I was playing. At first I didn't understand. Relax in the face of being judged? Relax with the threat of rejection hanging over me?

"Think of what makes you happiest, Lang Lang, and then play."

I thought of Monkey King, of Tom and Jerry, of kids I played with on the air force base, of my Transformers. I thought of my mother but not my father. The more relaxed I felt, the better I played. I came to love Professor Zhu almost as much as my mother. Every week I went home with a new exercise book and a new composition to learn. My father, when he picked me up, asked her why I wasn't assigned two books and two new compositions. Professor Zhu always held her ground and usually won the standoff.

After a full year of lessons, my father stunned me one evening with a bold proclamation. He said I was ready for my first competition. There had been vague talk in our house about my future career and the importance of competing to get ahead, but at age five? Professor Zhu reluctantly agreed. I was young, she told my father, but she didn't doubt my talent or determination. Every year Shenyang held a citywide competition for all piano students under the age of ten. Professor Zhu told me to expect no less than five hundred students to enter the competition.

It was agreed between Professor Zhu and my father that I would play a work by the twentieth-century Russian composer Dimitri Kabalevsky, a difficult piece that was sure to impress the judges because of its high degree of technicality. I went home and practiced many hours, and thought I had mastered the piece. However, one afternoon, playing for Professor Zhu, she told me I had the tempo wrong.

I began to cry. In my mind, I had already lost the competition.

"Don't be discouraged," she told me. "I can show you what you're doing wrong, and how to avoid those mistakes for the judges."

I bit my lip, gathering my composure. "Okay, Professor Zhu, show me."

Professor Zhu did exactly that. My face lit up when I understood how to play the correct tempo.

That night I practiced until my fingers throbbed. I knew the Kabalevsky piece would be challenging for someone even three or four years older than me, but I was determined to get every note and every musical nuance perfect. I have never run away from a challenge. In fact, the more I'm told something is impossible to do, the more I want to accomplish it. The harder I practiced the Kabalevsky, the more I looked forward to the competition. The prospect of winning began to dominate my fantasies night and day.

Whenever I needed a break, I went to the closet and pulled out my box of Transformers. When I played with them, I was like a general in charge of his troops, making the Transformers into one shape or another according to my battle plan. I was decisive in my games, not unlike my father.

Any other five-year-old might have been nervous and uncertain of his chances, but Professor Zhu as usual had a calming influence. And rather than rattle me, my father's prediction actually inspired me. "You will win this competition, Lang Lang. It doesn't matter there are children twice your age competing. You have practiced harder than anyone. You will win and be asked to join the Shenyang Conservatory. This is the first leg on your journey to fulfilling your dream. Number one, Lang Lang."

My father often spoke of "number one" this and "number one" that. To be number one in China was a goal, if not an obsession, of the entire country. People spoke of the number one tractor manufacturer, the number one gymnast, the number one painter, and the number one car mechanic. There was a local number one, a regional number one, a national number one, and I suppose a world number one.

Being number one was a goal that would come to give my life meaning, and provide great lessons when I fell far short.

{ 3 }

My memories of the actual competition are vague. My heart was hammering furiously in my chest—partly from excitement over the chance of doing well, partly in fear of making a mistake and disgracing myself—but I do remember most of the boys and girls there were taller and older than me. I was short and didn't want to look my competitors in the eye. It would seem impossible not to feel intimidated, yet I wasn't. As I waited for my turn to play, a competitor would walk out of the concert hall shaking his or her head and telling anyone who would listen, "I played terribly. Everyone is playing terribly. The judges are impossible to please. You might as well give up before you go in."

Parents were not allowed to wait with you—they were kept outside—but my father had already warned me about distractions. Before he said good-bye that morning, he gave me a reassuring pat on the back and some advice: "Do not listen to what anyone tells you, Lang Lang. Pay no attention to the other students. There is much jealousy. Just focus on what you're going to play. Be disciplined."

When my name was called, I marched into the hall, bowed to the judges, adjusted the bench, and poised my fingers over the keys. Monkey King was with me. He told me not to be afraid. When I had finished the Kabalevsky I knew I had played well. I had made no mistakes. But how had the others done? How fair were the judges?

The results were announced the next day. When I learned that I had placed number one out of almost five hundred competitors, I was elated. My mother hugged me with joy, and Professor Zhu beamed with pride. My father, however, never even managed a smile.

"Congratulations," he said, looking at his watch. I knew what he was thinking. He didn't have to tell me. I marched straight to my piano.

I was disappointed. Wasn't winning the competition what we had all worked so hard for? Why couldn't we celebrate, even for a day? But it was clear my father was focused only on the future. "Do not get carried away with your victory," he said later. "You will now be going to the Shenyang Conservatory. That is a necessary first step.

But what it means, Lang Lang, is you must work even harder."

I often wondered what, if anything, made my father truly happy. Was it my mother? His pride in me? The joy of music? Or his all-consuming dream that I become the best pianist in the world? On weekends he would sometimes play the erhu, alone, not realizing I was observing him. He played with technical perfection, but the music always sounded sad, as if he was mourning the career he never had, or he was reminiscing about a time that had never actually existed.

If he caught me watching him, he would say, "Lang Lang, why are you wasting your time? Go to your piano. Learn! Learn!"

So I did. Professor Zhu was still my private teacher, and whatever she asked of me, I always tried to give her more. Whenever I felt my father was too overbearing, I would turn to my mother for comfort, and to my imaginary world of Monkey King, Tom and Jerry, Donald and Daisy Duck, or my beloved Transformers. I was also introduced by my air force base friends to Spider-Man and Superman and many kung fu masters. All of these became material for the stories that populated my imagination.

I was also intrigued by the biographies of composers I heard about at the conservatory. I had lots of questions for my father and Professor Zhu.

"Of all the famous composers, who is number one?" I asked my father one night.

"Mozart," he replied without hesitation. "Mozart is number one. He began playing the piano when he was two, creating his first composition, Andante in C, before he was five. Mozart was a supergenius who wrote and played everything—concertos, symphonies, chamber music, chorales, and operas. He wrote for princes and kings in the courts of Vienna, Austria. His father, Leopold Mozart, watched over him and helped bring his music to the world. Were it not for Mozart's father, he would not have become famous. Together, they achieved immortality."

Even at age six, I understood the meaning of my father's message, and to please him I pushed myself even more, but with a child's imagination. I envisioned Mozart as a character in a cartoon, skipping and running, chasing his friends around the playground. Unlike the gray, cold, and polluted skies of Shenyang, I saw Vienna as a paradise of golden light and Mozart as the golden boy who danced from one birthday party to the next, entertaining everyone. I wanted to be just like him, except I wanted a long life. Wolfgang Amadeus Mozart died from rheumatic fever when he was only thirty-five.

As I learned to play the other great composers of history—Bach, Chopin, Beethoven, Tchaikovsky, Liszt—I made up personalities and fantasy adventures for each of them that allowed me to interact. In a sense, they became my companions. For example, when I saw Elvis Presley on television, I began to think of Liszt as a rock star like Elvis, enjoying the company of beautiful women, racing motorcycles, and flying jet planes. Unlike Mozart, Liszt did not die young. He found a way, maybe with the help of someone like Monkey King, to keep his music alive as he leapt from one adventure to another. His creativity fed his love of life, and in turn his adventures fed his creativity.

The purpose behind my rich fantasy life was to entertain myself when I played, but it was also an escape from school. I was shy and the object of classmates' ridicule; my teachers didn't understand me. Whenever I asked to leave school early to practice, they thought I was lying, peculiar, or both. Of course, I didn't do anything to make them feel otherwise. Rarely did I speak up in class; I didn't interact with other students. My courses bored me in comparison to what I was learning and accomplishing on the piano, so I often faded off into daydreams. My mother knew I struggled and tried to make me feel better, but when she talked to my teachers, their attitude didn't really change. I was an outsider because of my differences. There were days I wished I were anywhere but the prison I called school.

Then Mrs. Feng came into my life—at just the right moment. Chinese teachers are usually strict or indifferent to their students, but Mrs. Feng, no older than twenty-seven, was more like Professor Zhu—warm and personable, and beautiful as well. She had the ability to see behind my timidity, to reach a part of me that no one else had reached and bring me out of my shell—like a magician coaxing a rabbit out of a hat.

"Lang Lang," she said one day, "you must not be afraid to speak your mind. You must express what you know."

I didn't want to express anything except through my music. I was afraid of sounding stupid and getting ridiculed more than I already was.

Mrs. Feng wouldn't accept my self-doubt. "You're a bright boy, Lang Lang. Whatever you've accomplished musically, you can accomplish academically. Let everyone know what you think and feel."

"I'd rather not say anything," I said stubbornly.

"You have no choice," she replied, equally firm. "When I ask you a question, you must come to the front of the class and respond. Maybe you'll be uncomfortable at first, but you'll get used to it. You'll do fine."

As the year progressed I came to understand how right she was. At first I was exceedingly nervous in addressing the class, but soon I couldn't wait to tell everyone about my country's history and culture and the different arts of every dynasty. Mrs. Feng read us poems from the Tang Dynasty, from A.D. 618 to 904, an incredible period in Chinese history known as the Golden Era. I could imagine the warriors and workers and merchants, how they dressed, where they lived, what their families did. If I didn't understand a poem or lesson, I spoke up. Mrs. Feng was always patient in answering my questions. My classmates began to respect me for not being afraid to ask the questions that they wanted to.

I didn't realize just how much I needed attention and affection from Mrs. Feng, and from Professor Zhu and my mother as well, until I turned seven. I'll never forget the stern expression on my father's face after dinner one night when he made the announcement.

"Lang Lang," he said, "you are now ready for your next competition."

It was as if the event had already taken place, a mere formality that I had to get out of the way as I continued on with my young career.

{ 4 }

Was I ready for my next competition? I was practicing longer hours, tackling more difficult compositions, and Professor Zhu never hesitated to praise me for my progress and focus. I played my piano at home so often and hard that I broke many strings, maybe a hundred different times. When we had the money to pay for repairs, I was happy, but sometimes I had to play for weeks, even months without certain strings whose notes I would hear only in my mind. That made practice more challenging.

There were other changes that also distracted me. My father applied for and was accepted into the Shenyang

Police Department as a vice officer, in charge of security in the entertainment districts of the city. The pay was better than the air force, and he suddenly had the respect from fellow officers and the public he thought he deserved. But that didn't improve his disposition with me. If anything, he was more focused on my career than ever. Every other word out of his mouth to me was "practice."

We had to move from our air force barracks to an apartment in the city that wasn't as large or luxurious. I lost track of my old friends, which I think was fine with my father, but my mother did her best to ease the sting by cooking my favorite dishes and spending more time with me. Still, my life was mostly centered on the upcoming competition. It was to be held in Taiyuan, the capital of Shanxi Province. The first contest had been local, but this one was national. I would be competing with students from all over China.

"Are you nervous?" asked my grandfather a few days before the competition.

"No, I'm fine."

"Come here," he said, waving me over to the couch. My mother's dad had come over to our apartment to watch a performance by the Beijing Opera. I sat on his lap and he put his arms around me. I knew he was very proud of me. "Here is where your love of music comes from," he said, nodding to the images on the television. "Your mother only listened on the radio, but now we can *see* the costumes, the acrobatics, the dazzling swordplay . . ."

I watched, fascinated, as Grandfather explained the

stories that were the heart of every opera. This one was about revenge and love and fighting for your country.

"Do you hear how the stories drive the music and the music drives the stories?" he asked.

My imagination was racing, loving everything before me, and I did understand how the music and story related to each other. Since I was two or three and watched the cartoon with Tom and Jerry playing piano, their antics in perfect sync with the music, I had understood. "I do," I said. "I hear everything."

I was sorry when my grandfather had to leave. He wished me luck with the competition. My father came back from work, so I returned quickly to my poorly functioning piano.

Two days later, taking the train from Shenyang, we reached the Taiyuan station on a damp afternoon. My father was in high spirits. "You will win everything," he predicted. "You will take first prize."

"What is first prize?" I had been so focused on my performance I'd never thought about actual prizes.

"A brand-new piano."

My heart began to gallop. A new piano? This was a dream. No more busted strings, broken pedals, or daily prayers that nothing else bad would happen to the instrument I loved so dearly. A new piano would lift my spirits and allow me to play even better.

"Second prize," my father continued, "is an electronic keyboard. You don't want an electronic keyboard, do you?"

"No."

"Third prize is a television. We already have a television."

"I only want the piano. I want to be number one."

As we settled into our tiny hotel room, my confidence built. Only a month earlier, Professor Zhu and my father had accompanied me to some master classes in Shenyang, taught by American pianists from the Eastman School of Music. Twelve artists, twelve separate classes! It was my first time seeing and hearing Westerners play Western classical music. The average age of the students who attended was seventeen or eighteen, but I sat attentively, absorbing everything, asked questions when I could, and dreamed. One of my dreams was to be in the United States, attending a school such as Eastman, Juilliard, or Curtis, taught by teachers like these. Dreaming of that possibility in my dingy hotel room inspired me to want to win more than ever.

Professor Zhu had prepared me to play four compositions—a Mozart, a Czerny, a Bach, and a Chinese piece called "The Brilliant Red Star." I knew them backward and forward. The next morning, my father gave me his traditional pat on the back as I climbed the steps to the stage and looked out on the half dozen judges. Their faces were blank slates, but I wasn't nervous. I imagined Monkey King beside me as I scooted the bench closer to the piano and began to play.

I thought I played perfectly. So did my father. The judges, however, did not make me number one. Not even number two, or three, or four. I was awarded seventh place, and a consolation prize of a stuffed yellow toy dog. I was crushed, bewildered, outraged. In front of other kids and their families, I ran over to the judges and screamed, "It's not fair! You cheated me!"

I was having a seven-year-old's tantrum. I looked at the toy dog and kicked it into the air. The dog represented humiliation and defeat. I didn't want a consolation prize because I wouldn't be consoled by anything except victory. I knew the compositions that some of the winners had played, and they weren't as challenging as mine. I was so distraught and hot-tempered that my father had to take me by the hand and lead me from the auditorium.

On the train ride home I endured his stony silence. Was he giving up on me? Did he think I wasn't as talented as he had hoped? I continued to sulk, hating his silence almost as much as losing. As the train bumped along, I stared at the yellow dog as though it were a curse, an omen of the future.

The next day, in her studio, Professor Zhu put her arm around me. "You wanted to win very badly, I know. It's your nature to be competitive, Lang Lang, and that's a good thing. But you must know that the life of any artist is filled with disappointments. Look at your father's life, or mine. Setbacks are inevitable, and we must live through them."

"But I was cheated," I said. "I know how well I played."

"Lang Lang, what the judges decide is out of our control. Some judges *are* prejudiced, or have poor taste, or have an inferior ear. But most are fair and will recognize and reward talent. You can't stop entering competitions or give up on your career because you got a bad break. You must absorb this blow, as painful as it is, and come back strong. This is your first real test both as an artist and as a young man."

With that, Professor Zhu wiped away my tears and kissed my cheek. I loved her with all my heart at that moment, not just for putting everything into perspective but also for still believing in me. At school, Mrs. Feng was equally supportive. But my mother went one step further.

I was now practicing long into the night, determined never again to lose a contest. If that meant practicing when I could be eating or sleeping, or annoying neighbors who banged on our walls for me to be quiet, so be it. Nothing was going to stop me. My father was elated to see the fire in my belly. I kept the poor stuffed dog beneath my piano bench and kicked it whenever my old, beat-up piano broke another string.

"Lang Lang, you should not mistreat that dog." My mother spoke up one day.

"It's only a toy. And I wouldn't be kicking it if I had won a new piano."

"I think the dog is more than a toy. It will always remind you of something. It doesn't have to be defeat. It can remind you of how hard you're working to improve. It can say to you, 'I am your good-luck charm, Lang Lang. I will be with you next time you win.' "

Like Professor Zhu, my mother knew how to turn my

negative thinking positive. I thought about her words all night, and the next day I took the yellow dog and placed it on the ledge of the upright piano. Instead of a curse or bad omen, it became a token of good fortune. In China, almost everyone believes in lucky symbols, and for the moment I had found mine.

{5}

After I turned eight, I became aware of a certain amount of whispering between my father and mother and Professor Zhu. I was curious about what was going on, because clearly I was the subject, but no one wanted to say. Finally, alone with my mother in the apartment one afternoon, I confronted her.

"What is everyone saying?"

As usual, she knew what I was referring to. Still, she hesitated, as if the time to confide in me wasn't quite right because the issues, whatever they were, had not been resolved. "Professor Zhu says you are coming along beautifully. Faster, in fact, than any student she has ever taught."

"Not fast enough," I said.

"Plenty fast, but she's also a little worried."

"About what?"

"She thinks the musical world in Shenyang has its limitations. That you would do far better in Beijing. All the great teachers are there, Lang Lang."

"Professor Zhu is a great teacher. I don't want anyone else."

"But one thing that makes her great is that unlike many teachers in China, she does not put herself ahead of her students. Most teachers would never think of giving up a prize pupil like you, because a teacher's reputation is determined by her students. Professor Zhu recognizes that your growth and success come first. Her primary interest is for you to realize your potential. This can happen only in Beijing. If the rest of the world is ever going to know your talents, the door to that world is through the Central Conservatory in Beijing."

At first I was excited, not just by the chance to gain national recognition, but also by the thought that the three of us would be together on a great new adventure. I would miss Professor Zhu terribly, but as long as I had my mother and father, life would be fine. "We would all go?" I asked, to be sure. "You, Dad, and me?"

"Your father and I are discussing that."

"What do you mean?"

"There is the issue of money and how we can support

41

your needs in Beijing. Neither of us knows anyone there, so how would we find jobs?"

"Could I go then with just you, Mom? Dad could keep being a policeman here. He makes good money."

"But your father understands music better than I do."

"When would I go?"

"You have to finish the school year here first."

"Then you and I would go live in Beijing?"

She saw a shadow of fear cross my face and pulled me closer to her. "There's nothing to be upset or frightened about. No matter who is with you in Beijing, we will protect you with our lives. Your father and I will sacrifice whatever is necessary to ensure your success."

The door suddenly opened and there was my father, knowing instinctively it was time to assert his authority.

"Why are you sitting on the couch?" he asked me, in case there was any doubt who was the ruler of our family.

"We're talking," my mother answered.

"Lang Lang should be practicing."

"He's already practiced for two hours."

"We agreed upon three."

"I'm going to practice the third. Or fourth, if that's what you want," I spoke up. My father's gaze hardened at the boldness in my voice.

"Then stop talking to your mother and go to the piano."

"You don't understand! Leave us alone to talk!" I heard myself screaming, and wondered where my sudden rage came from. Was I just upset about the possibility, if not certainty, of moving to Beijing without my mother? Or was my anger directed at my ever-inflexible father because of my need to have my own voice in our relationship?

Without warning, my father turned and marched to a closet where I kept my toys, including my precious Transformers. He grabbed the box and without looking at my mother or me, one at a time, threw the Transformers out the window. I ran to stop him, but he pushed me away.

"Guoren," my mother said, as shocked as I was, though she never lost her cool. "The boy has done nothing for you to be acting this way."

"He has defied me."

"They're my toys!" I screamed, trying to grab the box.

The louder I screamed, the faster my father flung my Transformers to their death. In my imagination I thought that somehow they were more than mere toys, and they could be saved by transforming themselves into steel or stone and none would be damaged.

When I ran downstairs, crying, I found most of them scattered in small parts around the street, broken beyond repair. One or two were miraculously in one piece. I hugged them to my chest, wondering if I was still in one piece too. Some inner voice—maybe an echo of Professor Zhu—told me I had to be strong.

When I went upstairs, I expected my parents to be in a fight, yet my father had calmed down and was speaking in a reasonable tone. I retreated to the next room, but I could overhear everything. It became evident my father had thought out his argument well in advance, and as usual he believed that logic would always triumph over emotion.

"In Beijing," he addressed my mother in a clear voice, "I must devote all my time to supervising Lang Lang. The conservatory is not an easy school for a child from the provinces. There are many adjustments to make and roadblocks to overcome, political ties to establish and nurture. Also, Beijing is a huge city with many distractions. Lang Lang needs a man to protect him."

"But we've never been apart. He is still so young."

"You'll visit whenever you can. It's not like you'll never see him again."

"Of course I want him to succeed, but . . ."

"We must do this. You must accept this. That's the way it is."

They continued to make their arguments, but after a while it was just words being volleyed back and forth. The strength and conviction in my mother were waning. She was no match for my father. As she dissolved into tears, my heart sank like the sun into the horizon. Logic and emotion, discipline and spirit, ambition and doubt—the contradictions that always ran through me under the surface had suddenly bubbled to the top. I felt paralyzed and uncertain. I didn't want to leave home without my mother, but just as Xiulan's voice had been silenced by my father's will, I too understood there was no choice.

BEIJING, 1991–1997

{6}

When my mother and I arrived in Beijing early in the evening, we were both tired and hungry. The train ride from Shenyang had taken twelve hours, and neither of us had slept much. I had been preoccupied with thoughts of my friends and family, wondering when I would see them again, but those ruminations were abruptly whisked away by what unfolded in front of me. Not only was I staring at the largest, busiest train station I could possibly imagine, but beyond it I glimpsed an unending city of motion and noise that seemed to stretch into the horizon. Once more I was frozen in place.

Where was my father? We kept looking vainly through the bustling crowds. I could see my mother was worried. Finally, I spotted my father coming toward us with his stern, purposeful gaze. I had hoped for a hug or at least a handshake of welcome, but he simply said, "Come, I'll take you to our apartment."

The bus ride seemed interminable, snaking through one traffic jam after another, one neighborhood after another, and everyone talked a mile a minute. I could barely understand them with their accents. No one smiled or seemed to pay us any attention. I complained to my mother that this wasn't another city in China, it was like another world.

"I know it must be a shock, but you'll get used to it, sweetheart," she promised.

We finally arrived at my new neighborhood, Feng Tai, which to my eye was little more than a slum. The smell of garbage and animal urine made me nauseous. Apartment houses looked as if they were ready to topple with the slightest earthquake. How could I live here? How could I relax and play my best music? I hated what I saw with all my heart.

My mother sensed my despair. "As soon as things improve for us, Lang Lang, you'll be able to move to a better neighborhood."

I opened the door of our apartment, peeked in at the sparsely furnished, cramped space, and only grew more depressed.

"There's the piano," my father said proudly, nodding to the corner. "Now go practice."

"Guoren," my mother replied, "we've just come from

a long journey. We're tired and hungry. And Lang Lang was bedridden with a fever for two days."

"Because he was sick, he can't afford to miss practice," my father insisted. "He must practice two hours before going to sleep."

I obeyed my father because it was easier to play, even with tears in my eyes, than to listen to my parents bickering, or risk my father going crazy and throwing more of my toys off the balcony. It was easier to play and lose myself in fantasies of Monkey King than to deal with my feelings about my new home and being without my mother. To survive, I knew I needed Monkey King, or the new kung fu masters I had begun to read about, as my friends.

The next morning, my mother fixed my breakfast, and when we were done eating she gave me a long hug goodbye. We both began to sob. When I wouldn't let go of her, my father grabbed me by my arms and pulled me away.

"Just go, Xiulan," he told my mother. "Go before it gets worse."

I don't know how long I was inconsolable after my mother's departure. It seemed forever. Most of that time I sat by my piano and practiced away the pain. In the morning, when my grief returned, I went straight to the piano and played for hours, until finally I could feel nothing but the music I was creating, and the lost worlds it inspired in my imagination.

A few days later, I was on the back of my father's rickety bike, splashing through puddles of rancid water while he weaved doggedly through a maze of pedestrians, bicycles, and cars. Despite having memorized directions to the conservatory, he was quickly lost and grew irritated. He pedaled frantically because he hated being late, especially to an appointment as important as this. I wanted him to slow down but was afraid to say so. I kept thinking: *What if we crash and I fall off the bike and break a bone in my hands?* My hands were the most important part of my body. Without them I had no career, no future. My father had told me this over and over, but he didn't seem to think about it now.

It took us two hours to reach our destination, twice the time it should have. I was exhausted.

"When you meet your teacher," he reminded me, "it's critical that you impress her. You must play perfectly. No mistakes. Do you understand? She's on the faculty of the conservatory, so if you win her support, her vote will help get you in."

I had never known a time when my father didn't expect me to play perfectly, so I was less bothered by the pressure of his expectations than by my cold, raw hands.

It turned out my new teacher was the exact opposite of Professor Zhu. She would prove to be more like my father—remote, judgmental, impatient, and demanding. I would come to call her Professor Angry. All the months I played for her, not once did she say I had talent or potential, or I was extremely advanced for my age, or I played with both emotion and technical skill. Professor Angry didn't believe in motivation through praise.

Still, I played well enough for her that morning to be accepted as her student.

"Why was she so angry with me?" I asked my father afterward.

"That wasn't anger, that was professionalism. She has no time to coddle you. You are almost ten years old, a young man. You must expect to be treated like a young man."

"I don't like her," I said as my father put me on the back of his bike and we headed home through worse traffic than in the morning.

Back in the apartment, life took on the usual regimen of unending practice. However, as fall gave way to winter, the cold was more severe than anything I'd experienced in Shenyang. Our apartment had no heating—none at all—and when I practiced I had to wear two pairs of pants, two shirts, and a scarf around my ears. I could see my breath in front of me. Only the intensity of my playing kept my fingers warm. Sometimes at night it was so cold I couldn't stop shaking. Wanting to be sure I got a good night's rest, my father would crawl into the bed before me to warm it up.

Mother regularly sent money and long letters from Shenyang, and I always wrote back begging her to visit. My father couldn't cook to save his life, I wrote, and every night the cold in the apartment felt unbearable. I knew that if she were there, just her voice and her eyes would warm me up.

She didn't come once the entire winter, though I know she badly wanted to. She was too busy working as many hours as she could, making money for us to survive. My father, always a man of few words, provided little companionship, and even though I ran into kids at the conservatory whom I'd known in Shenyang, they were as cold to me as the fierce weather.

"Why are my old friends avoiding me?" I complained to my father.

"I don't know. Maybe they are jealous of you. Maybe they think you will make them look bad."

"But they were so friendly in Shenyang."

"Beijing is not Shenyang. Beijing changes people."

I wondered if it would change me too. I didn't want to become someone who turned his back on old friends. "It bothers me."

"Don't worry about them. Just worry about practicing. You aren't practicing enough."

At first I practiced until seven in the evening, then, goaded by my father, until eight, then nine, then ten and eleven. Neighbors would bang on the walls and shout for me to stop. My father didn't care and ordered me to keep playing. After a few weeks, the police showed up at our door, threatening us if I didn't stop making a racket. I felt they wouldn't know Beethoven from "Chopsticks," but I kept quiet. Only because my father had been a policeman in Shenyang and quickly offered newspaper clippings as proof of his fine reputation did they show us some leniency. My father explained how urgent our situation was. I was a prodigy and my future depended on gaining entrance to the conservatory. I *had* to practice. He finally won their sympathies, and they agreed that I could play until a reasonable hour in the evening, as long as I agreed not to start too early in the morning. They told the neighbors to stop complaining.

Professor Angry didn't make my life much easier than the neighbors. One afternoon she gave me a difficult piece by Beethoven. She warned me to play the piece "delicately, not heavy-handedly." I practiced at my apartment until my fingers and hands were numb. As I rode the next day on the back of my dad's bicycle to Professor Angry's house, I went over the piece in my mind, note by note. I wanted to show her how I had mastered it.

At her house, after barely playing a page, I was ordered to stop. Professor Angry's voice was impatient, even nervous. "You're playing Beethoven like you're afraid of him. You're playing it too light."

"You said for me to play it delicately," I reminded her.

"No, I didn't."

I was stunned, but I knew better than to argue and make her even angrier. My father had been out of the room for the last lesson, so he didn't know what she had said. But I did.

I took a calming breath and resumed playing, but she stopped me almost instantly.

"Too light," she said again. "Too tentative. You must approach this with a heavier hand."

"But Professor—"

"Don't 'but' me. You must pay attention to my directions or I can no longer teach you. You play like a samurai."

"What does that mean?"

"You play like someone who is fighting a battle. You play like water—no taste. You should think about Coca-Cola and have some taste. You need to find that by yourself. Your spiritual feeling is like you are a farmer in a potato field." She obviously didn't like the poor farmer either.

Professor Angry went on to tell me how music and records by Schnabel, Rubinstein, Horowitz—everything Western—had been destroyed during the Cultural Revolution.

At this point my father rushed into the room to take the side of Professor Angry. He apologized to her that I wasn't prepared, and promised that next time I wouldn't be so lazy. I was shocked that he didn't speak up for me.

Outside, after the lesson, I jumped on the back of my father's bike and held on to his waist. I just wanted quiet, but he began lashing into me as we started home. "She is your teacher and the only way you're getting into the conservatory! Do you understand?"

"She's crazy," I countered, "and a liar."

My father pedaled like a maniac, more erratically than usual. "You are ruining your chance for success!" he screamed, turning his head to look at me. "You are stupid and lazy."

"I'm not!" I yelled back, tears streaming down my face, and the wind biting my eyes.

"You're not trying hard enough."

"I can't try any harder."

"Then you are a fool," he answered.

He stopped listening. Furious, he jerked the bike to the right, veering from the bike lane into a car lane. I lost my grip, and my head was suddenly dangling inches from the street. I bumped along like a piece of cargo that had come untied, half on, half off the bike. If my father hadn't reached around for me at that instant, allowing me to grab his jacket sleeve, I would have tumbled into the traffic.

In the apartment, when I'd recovered from my scare, I practiced a Beethoven piece according to Professor Angry's latest directions, hoping to please her. But I was afraid I was being set up for something. My father had been brainwashed and couldn't help me. I could barely hold down my food before the next lesson.

"You're still not playing this right," Professor Angry said harshly as my fingers glided over the keys. "Something is missing."

"What's missing?"

"You don't know? Then how can you become a great artist? Your playing lacks passion."

Again I bit my tongue. Since I was four years old I'd been playing with the passion of a much older student. Even in my competitions, the judges had remarked on this quality as much as they had praised my technical abilities. Passion was my hallmark.

I started the piece again, carefully interpreting every stanza. Professor Angry stopped me once more.

"You're not listening to me."

"I'm trying."

Then my father intruded. "Don't talk back to your professor!"

My hands were now shaking, and I made a series of mistakes as I continued to play. Professor Angry would barely look at me. The more she criticized me, the crazier it made my father. Over dinner that night, he accused me of not just letting myself down but also bringing shame to my entire family. In China there are few things worse than disgracing your parents. I longed for my mother, both to be consoled by her and to beg her to talk sense into my father. Most of all I needed someone to tell me not to give up, because I had a novel feeling rising in my belly. I wanted to surrender. I wanted to give up the piano.

My mother's spring visit to Beijing, while providing me a boost of confidence, didn't completely ease my doubts and loss of spirit. My mother cooked for us, and it was wonderful to taste her delicious dumplings and other flavorful dishes. And finally I was able to confide in her about Professor Angry. For whatever reason, I told my mother, my teacher was not on my side. She was out to get me.

Before my mother returned to Shenyang, she made my father promise to watch how diligently I practiced, day and night. He finally admitted to me what my mother had always known, that I couldn't be working any harder, and Professor Angry was wrong to accuse me of laziness.

Yet my father was hesitant to criticize her. In China, teachers, especially professors, were like gods. My father had always believed teachers were somehow above scandal or bias, particularly Professor Angry, whom he considered number one.

The next week, as usual, my father and I bicycled to the professor's house despite a rainstorm, which is typical of Beijing spring weather. I should have interpreted the weather as an omen. By the time we reached her house, we were both soaked to the bone. Inside, I shivered from the cold, yet neither my father nor I was offered a towel or hot tea.

"If you'd let us dry off, Professor," said my father, "Lang Lang can start playing for you."

"That won't be necessary," she replied.

"Why not?"

"I've decided to no longer teach your son."

I felt tears welling in my eyes. When I glanced at my father, his face had paled. Words seemed to elude him, but it wasn't hard to imagine his despair. This could not be happening, he was thinking, because there was no other teacher for his son, no other path for me to enter the conservatory.

"I don't understand," he finally uttered. "My son is a genius."

"Most parents of children like yours are terribly biased. They think their children are geniuses. One can forgive them for their pride, but in the end we must all be rational. Not only is your son far from a genius, Lang Lang does not even have the talent to win admission to the conservatory. My suggestion to you and him is to go back to your home city and do something else. He will never become a pianist."

"What?"

"I'm afraid it's a lost cause."

"In Shenyang he is famous."

"Shenyang is not Beijing."

She had used my father's own words against him, and he was dumbstruck again. He gasped for words like someone trapped without air. "You must reconsider, Professor. We are betting everything on my son's talent. We live modestly in Beijing in order to afford your fees."

"I'm sorry, Lang Guoren, but my mind is made up."

Professor Angry turned without a good-bye or even a parting glance at me, as if I had been a problem since the day I showed up. Still soaked from the storm, we drifted back out into the rain. I couldn't stop crying as I cinched my arms around my father's waist and he pedaled silently home. My life as a musician was ruined. In an instant, my future had collapsed. While my father didn't say a word, I felt the pain of having let him and all of Shenyang down. We were shocked. We were both devastated. I was ten years old.

{ 7 }

My father had always stirred deep emotions in me. On one hand, I respected him for his strict work ethic— indeed, I imitated it—and I was sympathetic for what he and his parents had endured under Mao's government. Also, I had grown dependent on his daily approval and on his structuring of my piano practices. But part of me had begun to fear him, and also worry for him. With our latest setback, with Professor Angry, he seemed more desperate than ever for our success.

I couldn't wait for my father to find another teacher for me, even if he or she wasn't "number one." Until then,

I would be totally at the mercy of my increasingly moody father. If Professor Angry represented number one, I thought, I would be happy with number two or three, anyone who believed in me and my chances of entering the conservatory. My mother had written that Professor Zhu was in the United States for six months, traveling and teaching. I told my father that he should contact her. Surely she would have names of good teachers in Beijing.

My father seemed hesitant to take my recommendation. Was he already talking to other teachers? What was he thinking? I had no clue because he communicated very little to me and spent more and more time alone. Since we couldn't afford a phone in the apartment, I wasn't even sure if he'd told my mother about Professor Angry.

As I grew more afraid of my father, I tried to avoid him whenever possible. At home, piano was both my escape and a way to keep my father off my back. "Practice until your fingers ache" was one of his commands, and my cue not to confront him. I sensed his new goal for me. I had to attain such a level of perfection that no one could reject me, or him, ever again.

After school, rather than running home to practice, I had begun playing piano for the student choir. My father begrudgingly gave permission because at least I was doing something with the piano, even if it wasn't the demanding compositions I played at home. To my delight, I was praised by both the choir conductor and the students. I badly needed some kind of recognition after Professor Angry's rejection.

One afternoon, the choir rehearsal went on for an extra ninety minutes, and I was very late getting to our apartment. From the street I saw my father leaning over the window. I could feel his brooding presence, hovering over the street like a sentry. When he finally spotted me from his perch, he began to shriek. "Where have you been? You are late! You can't be trusted! You have ruined your life and mine too!"

He was in a frenzy, acting like a crazy man. He was in no mood for what he called my excuses. "You've missed nearly two hours of practicing, and you can never get those two hours back. It is too late for everything. Everything is ruined!"

"It's not my fault," I said. "The choir needed me to stay late."

"You're a liar and you're lazy! You're horrible. And you have no reason to live. None at all!"

I felt a tremor through my whole body. "What are you talking about?"

"Dying," he said. "You should die! Everything is lost! You can't go back to Shenyang in shame. Everyone will know you were not admitted to the conservatory. They will know your teacher fired you. Dying is the only way out!"

His voice shook with rage. I began to walk backward, thinking that as soon as I reached the door I could turn and flee for my life. As if he knew my plan, he seized my arm and pulled me toward him. There was no escaping. He had his own idea of my fate.

"Take these pills!" he demanded, handing me a bottle

of strong antibiotics. "Swallow all thirty pills right now and you will die! Everything will be over. Count yourself lucky that you don't have to live in shame!"

For the first time in my life, I began to curse my father. Hatred came from my heart and out of my mouth, an un-ending stream of anger and bitterness that replaced my fear. Years later I would realize that my hatred was di-rected not at my father but at someone posing as my father. The man I was confronting was not my flesh and blood. He was a stranger, possessed by the demons of a past that he could never change.

I ran toward the balcony, eluding his grasp. When he came after me, I started kicking his shins as hard as I could. With my back to the balcony, I was suddenly afraid he would throw me to the street, as he'd done with my Transformers.

"Stop it!" I screamed. "You're acting crazy! I don't want to die!"

I dashed back into the apartment, but he chased me. "If you won't jump, then swallow the pills! Swallow every last one! I'll pry your mouth open and pour them down your throat!"

What I did next I can't easily explain. Maybe it was in-stinct, maybe intelligence, maybe just desperation. What-ever guided me, I tore myself from my father's grip and started hammering the wall with my fists, like a boxer at-tacking a punching bag. I told myself to pulverize the wall until every bone in my hands was broken. My whole life my father had taught me to protect my hands at any cost.

My hands were my future. Now, driven by my own rage and hopelessness, I thrust one fist after another into the unyielding wall. My knuckles began to bleed. Pain spiraled through every muscle and sinew. I didn't care.

Suddenly my father screamed, "Stop, Lang Lang! Stop!"

His glazed stare fell away, and I was suddenly looking into the eyes of my real father. I had shocked him back into reality, into the perspective of why we were in Beijing and what we were trying to accomplish. He reached out to examine my hands, to see how much damage I had done. Fortunately, I'd stopped before I'd broken any bones.

He hugged me and collapsed in tears. "I don't want you to die," he said softly. "I only want you to practice."

I'd never seen my father apologize for anything or to anybody, unless it was to a teacher or someone who could advance my career. He'd never apologized to me or my mother for his inflexibility and closed-mindedness. But there was no forgiveness in my heart. A fresh surge of anger overcame me as I recalled the years of abuse my mother and I had suffered. *No more,* I thought suddenly. Everything my father stood for—sacrifice, hard work, and discipline, virtues I normally prized—I was now against. There would be no more practicing, I told him. No more taking orders. No more conversations about finding a teacher or entering the conservatory. No more Mozart, Chopin, or Beethoven. No more piano, period. I hated him for making me hate music and the piano.

I was ten years old, but I had never had a childhood that was anything but a miserable effort at trying to be an adult.

My father stood there, sullen and speechless. I swore to him that everything was going to change and there was nothing he could do about it. He was no longer in charge of me. I didn't wait to see his expression. I simply turned and marched out of the apartment.

{ 8 }

If I'd been slightly older or braver, I would have immediately hitchhiked back to Shenyang and my mother. I felt I desperately needed her, but I didn't have money to make a phone call, let alone buy a train ticket. Over the next few days, I suspected that my father had spoken to my mother, telling her I had given up on the piano, but I sensed he had skipped the details. To admit he had almost thrown me off the balcony or poisoned me would have shamed him, just as he had accused me of shaming him and my family by disappointing Professor Angry. But I didn't ask what he'd told my mother. We weren't talking.

At lunch or dinner I ate with my back turned to him. We were two strangers living under the same roof.

I had adopted a new attitude toward my father. In my own way I was becoming just as inflexible as he was. Here is the list I kept in my head:

Never practice the piano.
Never play the piano.
Never even look at the piano.
Never speak to my father.
Never even look at him.
Never forgive him.
Never stop hating him. Hate him every hour,
minute, and second. Hate him for wanting me to
die. Hate him for not believing me when I told
him it was the choir teacher who made me late.
Hate him for making me hate the piano because I
always loved the piano, ever since I saw Tom
chasing Jerry across the keyboard, since I first
heard beautiful melodies and chords and
harmonies and understood the magic of music.

At school, the choir teacher asked me why I was no longer willing to play the piano. Everyone was counting on me, she said. I felt bad for disappointing her, but I was too ashamed of my father to tell the truth. Maybe I was also ashamed of myself for giving up. I made an excuse to the teacher and disappeared down the hall. I wanted to disappear from the planet. I tried to forget I had ever played the piano. Concentrating on school, on anything, was difficult because I was so miserable. My father had inched his way back into his old routine, pestering me about practice, as if he couldn't accept I had given up on my talent.

"You need to start practicing again, Lang Lang. You're forgetting everything you've learned," he said one evening.

In the old days I would have jumped at his command, but now I just walked away. He no longer had authority in his voice because he was so filled with shame. Yet I knew he had a point. The piano isn't something you give up for a period and then start up again, picking up where you left off. I knew Chopin and Liszt and Rachmaninoff had never stopped practicing. It was too dangerous to take your skills for granted.

I was tempted on many occasions to play again, but as the weeks and then months rolled by, I don't remember one day that I didn't feel hatred for my father. He would tell me that my mother was working long hours to support us, as if to make me feel guilty, but that would only feed my anger. *Supporting us for what?* I wondered. *Why are we still in Beijing?* I wasn't playing anymore, and my father didn't have a job. Why couldn't my mother at least visit us? I blamed my father for keeping her away.

Almost every night at dinner he would look at me with sad, frustrated eyes. The words out of his mouth were always the same: "Lang Lang, will you start practicing now?"

I didn't bother to answer. Playing was the only thing I found comfort in, but I could not play.

By summertime, I had not played for three months. With time on my hands after school, I began to wander the ancient streets of my *hutong,* or neighborhood, even though my feelings for Beijing were no kinder than they were for my father. But there were nice people here and there, willing to talk to me, including a fruit vendor in the outdoor market. I was hungry as I stared at the pile of melons in front of him, wishing I had some spending money.

"The way you're caressing that melon," the fruit vendor commented, watching me, "it's as if you're playing a musical instrument. Most people just poke at it."

"I used to play the piano," I said.

"What is your name?"

"Lang Lang."

"Ah, a beautiful name. You used to play? You look too young to be retired," he said with a smile that put me at ease.

"A long story," I answered, unwilling to go into details. "I had a teacher who said I wasn't very talented."

"Teachers can be wrong. I think you must play beautifully."

"How do you know?"

"I can hear you in my imagination. And I look at your hands and fingers."

My face must have clouded over with doubt, because suddenly he handed me a watermelon, as if it were his job to cheer me up. I told him I had no money.

"This watermelon is not for sale. I was saving it as a gift for a great musician. This is your reward for having practiced so long and hard. This is your prize."

He introduced himself as Han. I liked him immediately, not just because of his gift of the watermelon but also because he seemed to intuit so much about me. More than ever I needed someone to tell me that I still had talent and a future. Han had a solid build and honest eyes. He had such a warm personality.

I wasn't the only one to begin visiting Han regularly at the market. After I brought home the delicious watermelon, I spoke to my father for the first time to tell him about Han. My father was so pleased that he decided to buy all of our vegetables and fruits from Han. Soon my father was inviting him to our apartment for dinner. Han said he would come only if he could have the honor of preparing our meal. He turned out to be an incredible cook. To find someone who prepared food as delicious as my mother's was a surprise. It almost felt as if my mother had performed long-distance magic, somehow sensing my needs and sending Han to look after me.

Han, whose family was from the countryside, had come with his brother to Beijing. He too was a "foreigner" like me and my father. He'd left behind his son and wife to come make money in the city. He had studied martial arts. He had dark skin because he was always under the sun. He quickly became a member of our family—I began calling him "Uncle Number Two"—serving an important role in our household besides being the occasional cook. With his easygoing personality, Han was a buffer between my father and me, someone we both liked and could talk to separately or together. He sensed the friction between us but diplomatically kept his distance, as if he knew we would confide in him when we were ready.

"Lang Lang," he said after dinner one night, "I see your piano in the corner. Would you be kind enough to give me a small recital?"

"I would love to, Uncle Number Two, but I don't play anymore. I'm just a regular kid."

"I understand. I am a patient man. I will wait until you are ready."

"I will never be ready," I insisted.

"Lang Lang, never is a very long time."

Another month passed, and the sheet music on my piano was now regularly chewed by mice. Still I didn't play, even when I felt pressure that I should. The neighbor in our building who had called the police to stop me from practicing suddenly had a change of heart. He came to our door to tell me he now *missed* my playing, and begged me to start again.

At school, virtually every student in the choir signed a letter telling me how beautifully I played, and would I reconsider my decision not to join them. They were to enter a competition and needed me. The substitute they had found was not as gifted, and the whole choir was suffering. They also sent me a gift—a Transformer—to express their sincerity.

I did not tell my father about this letter. But when I told Han about the letter and the gift, he smiled broadly.

"Look how popular you are," he said. "Are you sure you don't want to start playing again?"

"I don't want to make my father happy."

"But why is this just about your father? Does it really make you happy to make him unhappy?"

I had finally leveled with Han about the falling-out with my father, including his threat to kill me, and that I was still very much afraid of him. "If he knows I'm playing for the choir, he'll get crazy all over again and tell me to either practice twenty hours straight or jump off the balcony," I complained.

"Lang Lang, I think you are misreading your father. He does not want you to suffer in any way. Perhaps it's time to forgive him. Anger is never a good thing."

"I don't trust him."

"Your father doesn't have to know you're playing for the choir."

"You won't tell him?"

He smiled in his calm, patient way. "My young friend, I'll not reveal your secret."

I hadn't played the piano in over three months, but I figured it couldn't hurt to drop by the school music room and look in as the choir rehearsed. When I walked by, everyone stopped and stared in disbelief. I was suddenly surrounded by the whole choir. They took me by the hand and led me toward the piano.

"Lang Lang's back!" one girl shouted. And everyone cheered.

What else could I do but play for them? When my fingers touched the keys I felt an immediate thrill. I realized not only how much I had missed my instrument but that Han was right about not staying angry with my father. Creating beautiful melodies chased away the bitterness in my heart and replaced it with my boundless love for creating music. I couldn't lift my fingers from the keys as I played the score handed to me by the music teacher at school, Mozart's Sonata in C Major (K330), second movement. As I played, I realized that my technical skills were rusty but that my heart had survived the three months off, that this had been a test of my love for my music and my heart was bigger than ever. I was so happy that afternoon that I could have played well into the night. I felt how much I missed playing the piano.

When I got home for supper, much later than usual, I concealed my joy and revealed nothing. I thought I had forgiven my father, but maybe not entirely. I was still afraid of him, still wanted him to feel as bad as he had made me feel.

Occasionally, when I was alone in the apartment, I would play a small piece, to lift my spirits, but as soon as I heard the front door open, I stopped.

"Lang Lang," he would say, "did I just hear you practicing?" His face lit up in anticipation that his most fervent prayer had been answered—until I shook my head. I gave him the silent treatment because I knew that added to his misery.

"I want you to answer me, Lang Lang!"

I turned my back and left the room.

A week later, wandering the street of my *hutong* and wishing I had money to buy the latest issue of *Dragon Ball Z,* my new favorite comic book, which was inspired by *Monkey King,* I felt a wave of despair. I was continuing to play piano at school for the choir, but it wasn't nearly enough to improve my skills. I stayed away from the more demanding pieces, almost afraid to tackle them without the help of a teacher. I knew I was falling behind. Any chance of gaining entrance to the conservatory, if that was still my dream, diminished by the day. I couldn't see a way out. Han had let me know that my stubborn father wasn't amenable to finding a teacher for me until I showed a willingness to start practicing again. It was a standoff and no one was going to win.

When I retreated to my apartment that afternoon, I heard a familiar voice as I approached the door. I listened again, disbelieving. *It can't be,* I thought as my heart accelerated and I threw open the door. But the voice was real, and so was the person standing in front of me, talking to my father. I ran up to Professor Zhu and threw my arms around her, crying. She was back from the United States and obviously had learned of my difficulties in Beijing, professional and personal.

"My dear boy," she said, "I know you've been sad."

"The teacher here said I had no talent," I cried. "Do I have talent, Professor Zhu?"

"Of course you do."

"But the teacher who fired me is a famous teacher in the conservatory and everyone believes what she says."

"She has made a serious mistake, Lang Lang. One day she will realize that. In the meantime, you must not think about her. You must think only about you and the piano and your future. We will find you another teacher."

In less than two minutes, Professor Zhu had restored the confidence and peace of mind that I had begun to lose when I boarded the train for Beijing. I hugged her again, not wanting her to leave.

"I haven't played seriously in over three months."

"I'll give you some brush-up lessons. It won't take long. Your talent hasn't vanished. Everything will be all right."

"When can we begin?" I said eagerly.

"Right now."

Over the course of the next hour she told me she'd already spoken to Professor Zhao Pingguo and his famous wife, Professor Ling, who was the head of the piano department at the conservatory, and had set up an appointment for me.

My father unfortunately mixed up the date, however, and I missed the right time. When I showed up, only Professor Zhao was there. I had missed the chance to play for his wife. He asked me why I had not shown up the previous afternoon. We apologized, and he allowed me to play for him.

My father stayed in the other room as I ran to the piano. In the next few hours I played my heart out, with not just Monkey King at my side but Professor Zhu as well. She praised and encouraged me as if we were back in Shenyang, and I felt a glow of confidence. At the end of the session Professor Zhao agreed to become my teacher.

That night my excitement was so great I couldn't fall asleep immediately. As I lay there I couldn't help overhearing Professor Zhu talking to my father in the next room.

"Tell me, what do you think really happened with his teacher?" she asked. "Why did she reject Lang Lang? Surely it couldn't have been for lack of talent."

"I have never told Lang Lang any of this," he said softly, almost sorrowfully.

"Told him what?"

"The professor was fed rumors about me, rumors that even though I was a policeman in Shenyang, I was connected to criminals, and she believed them. All she had to do was check the facts and she would have discovered it was false, but of course she never bothered to check. Since teachers prize their reputations, and their reputations are built on those of their students and their families, she decided it was best to get rid of anyone who might tarnish her image. Her rejection of Lang Lang had nothing to do with my son, only me."

"Who spread the rumors?"

"Pianist 'friends' from Shenyang. Jealous friends who didn't want to see Lang Lang in the conservatory. Friends who wanted their children to be the stars."

As I listened to my father, I began to cry again. Now I understood why he had not told me the truth. He was a man of such honor and pride that, despite his temper and impatience, he was determined to do everything possible to help me succeed. It was his entire reason for existence. To be the cause of my rejection by Professor Angry created in him the same feeling of shame and guilt as when he had threatened to poison me. It wasn't just my stubbornness that took the authority and confidence out of his voice; it was also his feelings about himself.

Professor Zhu also understood my father's emotions. She understood, as I was beginning to, that his way of motivating me might not be the best way, but it was the only one he knew, and he was incapable of change. I knew his intentions were pure.

"Lang Guoren, listen to me carefully," she said. "Professor Zhao is a good man and teacher and he will train your son well. I fully expect that within a year Lang Lang will be accepted into the conservatory. He has too much talent not to be accepted. But his struggle, your struggle, will not end there. Other students and their parents will be jealous. Judges at competitions have their favorites too. Parents with wealth and connections have a great advantage. You and your wife have only your tenacity and desire to protect your son. You must closely watch everything that happens at the conservatory. Take nothing for granted. Make sure Lang Lang is never put in a situation that compromises his potential or his future. Do you understand?"

I had never heard Professor Zhu speak with such earnestness and concern. I felt her love for me shining through every word. "Alone," she added, "I'm not sure Lang Lang can find his way through the maze, but with you by his side, he has a very decent chance."

"I'm there," said my father proudly. "I'm by my son's side. Nothing and no one can push me away."

{9}

I worked with my new teacher, Professor Zhao, for the next nine months, through fall, winter, and spring. My audition for the conservatory would take place the following summer, when Professor Zhao thought I would be ready for the rigorous and competitive entrance exam. My father, pleased with the professor, had regained his old confidence, talking again about my being number one.

"If your son gains admission to the conservatory," Professor Zhao said that first fall, "it will be victory enough."

"Short of number one," my father countered, "there is no victory."

*   *   *

By now my father and I had reconciled, at least in terms of my goals. I wanted what he wanted. For all the differences in our personalities and sensibilities, we shared a single obsession: for me to be the very best at the piano, to be number one. I would make any sacrifice toward that end, and he knew it. We were a team now. Yet in many ways the joy the piano brought me was childlike. I don't know if I could have played as well if I hadn't believed in the protective powers of Monkey King. And I imagined that I, like my Transformer toys, could transform myself into whatever figure I wanted, depending on the tempo and mood of the piece I was playing. My head was filled with wondrous fantasies and a joy that elevated my soul.

I liked my new teacher. Professor Zhao was a handsome man in his late forties, with swept-back black hair, and he was always elegantly dressed. He had a wonderful smile. He never yelled. He was open and encouraging. My first impression was that he looked like the host of a television show. He'd studied Russian and was steeped in the music, teaching methods, and composers of that culture. He was mellow and soft-spoken and never threatened me.

"Lang Lang," he would say encouragingly, "you're still too anxious when you play. Technically you are close to perfect, but you must relax and let the music come to you. Let it come *through* you. Music is not something to be conquered. Don't hold your breath. Lower your arms when you play. Take it easy. Relax."

He had only to watch my father watching me to understand why I could be so uptight. Little by little I got used to the idea of relaxing. Even Uncle Number Two noticed a change in my playing and in my demeanor.

"My teacher is nice, but I still have nine more months of hard practice. I can't relax completely. My father wouldn't like that."

"I've noticed your father is trying to show his love for you, Lang Lang. Be patient and accept it, and you will learn to give love back. Right now you love your piano and your music. But you will learn to love people too."

My father *was* trying to be my friend. Between my practice sessions, it was his suggestion that we play Ping-Pong—but we hit the ball against a wall because we couldn't afford a table. Then my dad's brother's son, Yifeng, who was six months younger than me, came from Shenyang to live with us. He played the clarinet, but not with the same enthusiasm or dedication as I had for the piano. He was a happy-go-lucky kid and we became good friends. Like Professor Zhao, Yifeng was constantly reminding me to relax. To a degree I did, but whenever my father felt Yifeng was being lazy and a bad influence on me, he yelled at him the way he used to yell at me. I would hurry back to my piano.

As fall turned to winter, my lessons with Professor Zhao became more frequent, and so did my sessions at home. I tackled increasingly complicated concertos and sonatas and demanded yet more complex and advanced pieces from Professor Zhao. I was happy with my progress and so was my father. The only hole in my heart was for my mother. With the Chinese New Year coming, I wanted to see her. While her letters from home cheered me, they were no substitute for an actual visit.

"Can't we go home for a few days?" I asked my father.

"All that time on the train will mean missing practice."

"Then why can't Mother come here?"

"She can't afford to miss work, not even for a day. And if she did visit, she'd only distract you and make you soft. She'd make you weak with sentiment. Now more than ever, Lang Lang, you must resolve to be tough."

Even Han was going to go home to his wife and son. When I visited him at the vegetable market, I complained that my father would not let me visit my mother or allow me to go home for the new year.

"Can you get my father to change his mind, Uncle Number Two?"

"I'm afraid not, Lang Lang. He is a stubborn man. Imagine this: you are a prizefighter, and when a prizefighter trains, nothing can be allowed to distract him. Do you understand? Have you seen the American movie *Rocky*?"

I told him I didn't see many movies, so Uncle Number Two smiled as he described the movie plot and its message of absolute dedication to your goal. My goal, to get into the conservatory, was like winning a prizefight. It required the same emotional and mental discipline as Rocky's. I told Uncle Number Two that I understood.

I went back to my father and made him promise that if I was accepted into the conservatory, I would be allowed to return home, and not for a short visit. I wanted to spend at least a month in Shenyang, even forty days. I would of course practice at home, but my main objective was to see my mother.

To my surprise, my father agreed.

As spring rolled into summer, I woke one morning with the realization that the conservatory exams were exactly one week away. To gain admission to the fifth grade, I would be competing against three thousand students my age from across China—students who had reputations greater than mine, more contest victories; and some who had a lot more money and connections. Only twelve would be accepted. For the next seven days my sessions with Professor Zhao reached a new pitch of intensity. Even in my dreams I was focused on the competition. Sometimes I dreamed I got in; other times I had nightmares of being kicked out in the first round. When I couldn't sleep, I got up in the night to practice. And when I did sleep, there were many more nightmares, including one where Professor Angry was judging an audition. I cried to my father. "She'll never admit me! She hates me! She doesn't think I have talent."

My father explained that it wasn't me that Professor Angry didn't like, it was him. She had believed the rumors about him.

"But she didn't like me either. She lumped us together. There's no way she's going to vote for me because she's already told the whole world I have no talent."

"Lang Lang, you're blowing this all out of proportion."

"When I filled out my application for the conservatory, you told me not to list Professor Angry as one of my previous teachers. I wrote down only Professor Zhu and Professor Zhao. Now I'll be caught in a lie and disqualified." When my father had applied to the Shenyang Conservatory twenty years before, he had written down his age incorrectly, and even though his was an honest mistake, the directors had used the technicality to disqualify him.

I broke into inconsolable tears. I was so anxious that my mind was racing a million miles a second. With the most important day of my life looming, I couldn't sleep. My father saw how agitated I was.

"Come to my bed," he said. "Sleep by my side."

When I crawled in next to my father, I asked, "Will you put your arm around me?" This was the first time in my life I had ever asked him for his affection.

"Yes, my son. I will put my arm around you."

In my father's protective embrace, I was able to turn off the noise in my head, and for the first time in days, I slept like a baby.

The next morning, I woke with the sun. I jumped with my father on his bike and we set off on our one-hour journey to the conservatory, dodging traffic all the way. The butterflies had returned to my stomach, but I tried to concentrate on the pieces I would play for the judges—Bach, Chopin's black key études, and a piece by the Russian composer Glinka, his "Nightingale" variations, that was one of Professor Zhao's favorites.

"Look at the line!" I exclaimed to my father when we reached the conservatory grounds. Hundreds of kids and their parents were already waiting to sign in. As my father and I joined the line, I felt so anxious that all I could do was summon the image of Monkey King. As always, Monkey King would be my protector. He would sit on the piano bench beside me as I played. He couldn't be defeated, and neither could I.

The line moved at a snail's pace and it kept growing. I was there for two hours, then three. Monkey King told me to push away my doubts, but I couldn't help thinking of the challenges I faced. Of the three thousand competitors, after the first round of playing, there would be forty survivors. For the second round, if I got that far, I would take a difficult written exam as well as play again for the judges. I was terrified of making a mistake of failure—despite my father's assurance that I would do fine.

When my turn finally came to enter the rehearsal hall, my father gave me the traditional pat on my back. I marched up onto the stage, stood erect by the grand piano, and bowed to the judges. I didn't dare look Professor Angry in the eye, but I sensed her staring at me with disapproval. Memories of enduring her lessons rushed into my thoughts, particularly the day she told my father and me to leave for good.

As I adjusted the piano bench and positioned my fingers on the keys, however, a great calm washed over me. Monkey King, who feared no one, was right beside me. My mind cleared. I began to play and nothing distracted me. For twenty solid minutes I played my heart out.

I was happy with the way I played and perhaps even happier to be done. The results wouldn't be posted for two days, so I largely spent the time wringing my hands and second-guessing my performance. Despite my father's and Uncle Number Two's repeated assurances that I would be among the forty finalists, I wondered what would happen to me if I wasn't. I was afraid that Professor Angry had spread her poisonous feelings for me to the other judges.

When I finally returned to the conservatory, I could barely breathe. In China, the tradition after a major exam or competition was to tack up on a bulletin board a piece of red paper with the list of winners in bold black ink. Spotting my name on that sheet of red, the Chinese color for good fortune, was a beautiful thing. I was one of the forty! Forty out of three thousand. I had escaped, at least for now, the wrath of Professor Angry.

Any joy was short-lived, however, as I prepared for the next phase of the audition. The forty finalists were given private rooms in the conservatory to rehearse their pieces. Because parents weren't allowed on campus, they would stand outside the gates and shout encouragement or advice to their kids as they practiced. Fortunately, my room was close enough to the gates so that my father could hear me play through the open window. He understood that the heart of my second round, a Bach sonata, required extraordinary sensitivity, and by calling out instructions to me, he helped me find that sensitivity. I needed all the help I could get. I was becoming increasingly aware of how important this moment was to so many Chinese families, who were staking their future on the success of their one and only child. It was do or die at age ten! As always, I tried to focus solely on my work, ignoring those kids who tried to psych me out. Everyone here was extremely talented, but like the prizefighter Uncle Number Two had described, I knew that only the mentally tough would survive.

For my written exam, a teacher played a chord and, with my back turned, I had to name it correctly—a sixth chord, a seventh chord, a dissonant chord, an augmented chord. Then there was the ordeal of repeating a rhythm pattern. A judge demonstrated it once and I had to duplicate it perfectly. This went on for twenty nerve-racking minutes.

After a short break, I entered the concert hall, bowed to the judges again, and adjusted the bench. I had been practicing eight years in anticipation of these thirty minutes. Under my father's constant scrutiny, I'd averaged six to eight hours of practice or more a day. I must have practiced more than two thousand hours a year, or more than twenty thousand hours in my young lifetime. The numbers staggered me. How many athletes or other professionals had practiced so long and arduously by the time they were ten?

I played Bach and other composers for thirty solid minutes. My fingers danced over the keys. I was in a zone of pure concentration. When the auditions were over, I thought I had played my best. So did my father and Uncle Number Two. But my competitors had played well too.

That night, before the judges posted their results, my father and I rode back to our apartment. My mood had turned somber. I knew I had to place in the top eight finalists to win a scholarship; otherwise, my parents couldn't afford the conservatory. I was so anxious that when I went to bed, I asked my father if he would slip his arm around me again. "Yes, of course, my son," he said. Even so, I didn't sleep well. My fear of possibly having made a mistake played itself over and over in my head like an off-key note. I also had nightmares of being chased by dragons. Early in the morning, I was awakened by a violent thunderstorm that refused to end. There were so many omens that I didn't know what to make of them. As I rode on the back of my father's bike to the conservatory, the cold rain soaked us both.

Uncle Number Two was already waiting as I hurried into the main building, my heart racing. In the distance, on the bulletin board, I could see the telltale piece of red paper. I could see kids and their parents huddled around it, many of them crying from disbelief and disappointment. I let Han and my father rush ahead. I was too paralyzed to move. Seconds later, the voice of Uncle Number Two broke through the din.

"Lang Lang," he shouted, "you're number one!"

He and my father ran toward me. For the first time since we had moved to Beijing, some eighteen months earlier, I saw a smile break out on my father's face.

It wasn't as broad as mine. I began to jump up and down, then let out a scream of joy. To be sure this wasn't a dream, I hurried over to find my name in black letters on that red paper. I kept staring. Whatever Professor Angry had felt about my playing, the other judges had obviously not agreed. I was so happy I wanted to hug somebody. But when I did, it was Uncle Number Two, not my father. Then I sent a telegram to my mother to tell her my news.

{ 10 }

Winning the conservatory competition boosted my spirits, and not just because of my performance, or the scholarship I was awarded, or the fact that even my lessons with Professor Zhao would now be paid for. My greatest joy was that I would be allowed to return to Shenyang and see my mother and other relatives and friends.

"When can we go back to Shenyang?" I eagerly asked my father.

"Soon."

"When?" I pressed. I hadn't been home in two years.

"It can only be a short visit. Twenty days. And you

must practice every day in Shenyang. Four hours in the morning and four in the afternoon."

"I will practice," I said, "but you promised me forty days."

"There's something more important than visiting your mother, Lang Lang. It's the Xing Hai national piano competition, and we have to start getting ready now."

"What's the Xing Hai competition?"

"It will be held at the conservatory, just before your first academic term. Students your age and older, mostly from the conservatory and representing all parts of China, will compete. By winning Xing Hai, you will prove to everyone that finishing first in the conservatory auditions was no fluke."

I was still relishing my conservatory victory, while my father was focused on the future, as usual. Of course I knew that to advance my career I would have to enter a series of competitions, but he always sprang news like this on me without warning. There was never any discussion. I had no vote. But for now I said nothing. I just wanted to see my mother.

"I'll practice eight hours a day in Shenyang," I swore. "But I want forty days."

"Twenty," he insisted. "In Shenyang there are too many distractions. You will concentrate better in Beijing."

I was furious that he had broken his promise. To pacify me, my father said I could visit my friends and relatives for two hours every day. But how could I be sure he would keep his word?

*　　*　　*

The morning our train departed for Shenyang the sky was masked by huge thunderheads. When the storms hit there was no end to them, and for the next few days flooding in northeast China was widespread. Our arrival in Shenyang was delayed by two days. Only when I finally reached home did I understand how worried my mother had been. She'd feared we'd been swept away in a flood. I assured her I had been in no real danger. No sooner had we shared a long embrace and hot tea, however, than I began to feel feverish.

As my temperature spiked in the next twenty-four hours, my mother insisted that I be admitted to the hospital. I remember very little from this time, only some crazy dreams where Johann Sebastian Bach was speaking to me in Chinese. I also remember wanting to be cared for by my mother, who remained vigilantly at my side at the hospital. My father was there as well, but he seemed anxious not so much about whether I would recover but about when I would begin practicing again.

I recall him saying, "Lang Lang, you will get well and you'll be number one in the Xing Hai national piano competition." Another time he said that unless I won the competition I wouldn't be allowed to come home again and my mother wouldn't be able to come to Beijing. It was as if he thought my mother was the enemy of my career, that she only made me weak, while I knew the truth was the opposite: without her love I had no strength or chance of lasting success.

*   *   *

When I recovered from my fever, I enjoyed every free moment I had with my mother. I cried for hours when I had to say good-bye and board the train again.

Back in Beijing, however, there was little time for sentiment; there was little time for anything but practice and more practice. In addition to Professor Zhao, my father soon met other teachers at the conservatory that he liked and enlisted on the Lang Lang team. Because I had placed first in the conservatory audition, I attracted both negative and positive attention. I was careful to disregard jealous classmates and teachers, and keen to learn from new professors who liked me. One in particular, Mr. Zhang, was almost as new to the conservatory as I was. Besides that similarity, we liked each other instantly. Mr. Zhang added a depth to my practices that I didn't get from Professor Zhao. This young teacher had a good speaker system at his little dorm. He listened to everyone from Horowitz to Barenboim, all the greats. He explained to me the difference between the Russian and German schools. He helped me to become a professional listener, able to distinguish between interpretations of the same piece. We tried to adapt the sounds created on the great Steinway pianos to our broken-down Chinese-made upright pianos.

As the date for the Xing Hai competition closed in, I grew increasingly anxious. There would be six winners selected: three number threes, two number twos, and one number one. I learned that Yang, the boy who had won the competition in Taiyuan, where I had placed seventh and taken home the consolation prize of the yellow stuffed dog, would be playing the same composition as me—Czerny's Etude, op. 740, no. 31. I also learned that out of twenty students competing, I had drawn the second position, which meant that by performing early, I wouldn't be able to hear my competitors, so I wouldn't know how well I had to perform in order to win. Third and perhaps most alarming was that Professor Angry would be one of the judges. If she hadn't worked her black magic the first time, I told my father, she had another opportunity.

"You shouldn't waste your time worrying about her or anything else," he said. "Just practice and focus. You will be fine."

Eight hundred people flocked to the campus auditorium to hear the competition. I played the Czerny as well as a Chopin waltz, a Bach prelude and fugue, a Beethoven sonata, and a traditional Chinese piece. The applause from my father, Uncle Number Two, Mr. Zhang, and my cousin sounded weak in the huge auditorium compared to others who had armies of family members to applaud. When I listened to the other students play, I had doubts my performance was strong enough to really impress the judges. As always, results weren't posted right away.

The next night I was home in bed, half asleep, when I heard my father tiptoe into the bedroom. He turned on a light so I could see his proud face. "Number one," he whispered.

"What?"

"You are number one again!"

"Am I dreaming?" I had to ask.

"You are awake, and you have won."

Then I realized Mr. Zhang was next to my father. He approached and put his hand on my shoulder. "When the judges finally appeared," he said, "I first asked the woman you call Professor Angry who had won. 'Lang Lang,' she said. Then I asked if she had voted for you. 'Yes,' she replied. 'I had to. I could no longer deny Lang Lang's talent.' "

{ 11 }

After I won the Xing Hai competition, my father allowed my mother to visit us in Beijing. One of the first things she did was to take me shopping for a new Transformer.

"Sweetheart," she said, "I can't tell you how proud I am of you. You won a national contest. You were chosen as the best from a group of students who were mostly older. Remember when I first put you on the train to Beijing? I told you that in my heart I knew you would be fine. Well, you are better than fine, I think. You are on your way to still greater accomplishments."

"Did Father tell you?"

"Tell me what?"

"There's an international competition he wants me to enter. 'The national is nothing,' he said. 'The international is everything.' "

My mother paused. I could tell she was surprised, and might not even agree with my father's decision, yet she didn't want to oppose him. She wanted to present a united front with him, certainly in terms of my future.

"Your father keeps track of all these competitions. He knows which ones are best for you. I trust his decisions. So should you."

"But—" I started to say, before I remembered that despite our ups and downs, my father was my ally. Without him I wouldn't be where I was. When I walked into a competition and felt his pat on my back, I became a different person—braver, more focused, more confident. It was a ritual so ingrained in me that I doubted I could survive without it.

"But why can't you live with us in Beijing? Do you do everything Father says?"

"I don't need your father's permission to live with you, Lang Lang. In fact, nothing would make me happier. But I could never find a job in Beijing as good as the work I have in Shenyang. You need my money to further your career."

I accepted her explanation, but I had doubts. I didn't fully understand my parents' relationship; what I observed was that basically my father called the shots, just as he did in selecting the competitions I would enter. Neither my mother nor I had a voice.

I did know this: the China International Piano Competition would challenge me like no previous contest. It was open to anyone under eighteen years old, and I hadn't even turned eleven. Students would be playing extremely advanced pieces by Liszt and Rachmaninoff. They were also deep into Beethoven's late sonatas, while Professor Zhao was still teaching me the early ones. No one needed to remind me how much preparation I had in front of me.

But these were the kind of challenges that I gravitated to, the ones where almost no one except my mother and father, Uncle Number Two, and Mr. Zhang thought I had a chance of winning. I wanted to prove everyone wrong. Besides practicing even more hours every day and enlisting the help of my old friend Monkey King, I began reading books about mysterious kung fu masters, one of whom dominated each of China's eight regions. My imagination allowed me to identify each of my seven top competitors with a rival kung fu master. I called myself Piano Master of the Eighth Region, the King of Chinese Piano, and I was stronger and more powerful than all my rivals put together.

While these were simply the mind games of a ten-year-old boy, they worked magic for me. They brought passion to my playing and helped me concentrate. The night before the competition, nervous as usual, I had to sleep with my father's arm around my shoulder. Before I walked onstage the next morning, my father gave me the standard pat on my back. And once I was standing like a proud soldier next to the piano, bowing to the judges and audience, I invoked the name of the Piano Master of the Eighth Region.

When I finished, applause and shouts of "Bravo!" were lofted at me like fresh flowers on the stage. I felt all my practices had once again paid off. My father and Uncle Number Two were pleased as well. But when the judges voted, I came in fifth. I was stunned. How could this be? Did the judges have their favorites?

"Lang Lang, consider what you've done to date," Uncle Number Two tried to console me. "You placed first in the entrance auditions for the conservatory. You placed first in a national competition. And you scored fifth just now against some very talented pianists. You've come a long way in a short time."

Ultimately I felt vindicated by the fact that the four winners, who would compete in the next round, were all considerably older and had played more difficult pieces than I. As it turned out, none of them would advance any further in the China International Piano Competition, leading me to wonder if I could have done better. Gradually, I forgot the sting of the loss and continued to think of myself as the Piano Master of the Eighth Region.

My father, rather than reprimand me for not having practiced enough, was unusually preoccupied. By now I could recognize that gleam in his eye. There was another competition coming up—a chance for redemption, an opportunity to show the whole world how well I could play. This contest was truly international in scale, taking place in Germany, the hallowed birthplace of Beethoven, Bach, and Brahms. There would be students competing from around the world.

I was up for the challenge. The thought of visiting another culture, hearing another language, appearing before a panel of European judges—all this contributed to my excitement, and I practiced almost to a frenzy. "Number one," my father would say like a mantra when he tucked me in bed at night. "Number one," I dutifully repeated.

In reality, I had no way of knowing how difficult my journey abroad would be, and how much chance and circumstance play a hand in one's fate.

PART TWO
WORLDS BEYOND CHINA

{ 12 }

It was the summer of 1994 and I was now twelve years old. My body was beginning to grow, yet my appearance was still that of a pudgy youngster, and I was a shy boy who had an active fantasy life to compensate for a lack of social skills. While I was driven by my dreams, I let my father take care of the practical details of my life, including our trip to Germany. I thought this would be relatively easy, but I soon learned we had two major obstacles.

"We don't have enough money?" I asked one afternoon, after my father had finally admitted how expensive the trip would be. He had to buy plane tickets not only for himself and me but also for Professor Zhao, who wanted to make sure my skills were honed with last-minute practice sessions. My father agreed this was important. Other expenses would include hotels and travel within Germany. He anticipated that in the West nothing would be cheap.

The second obstacle was that we had to obtain visas from the German embassy. I knew nothing about passports and visas, but I learned quickly that having talent and entering an international competition didn't mean anything to the bureaucrat we faced one morning. He was quick to point out the rules. My father needed a regular job, and both of us had to have proper health insurance—the two requirements for a visa. We reacted to the news with stunned silence.

The embassy official might have been more lenient, I thought, if I had been one of the winners in the China International Piano Competition. Two of those winners, a pair of sixteen-year-olds named Zhe and Yu, were also going to Germany. They were considered the best young pianists in China, and the government was proud to sponsor them because it was felt they were likely to win. I learned that they had already received their visas.

Compared to Zhe and Yu, I was a nobody. I had my supporters of course—my parents, Uncle Number Two, Mr. Zhang, and Professor Zhao—but to most people I was too young to be given any chance at winning. Attending a conservatory farewell party for everyone headed to the competition, a well-known teacher had come up to me and shaken my hand.

"I'm glad you're going to Germany," she said. "But if I were you, I wouldn't expect to win."

"Why not?"

"You will never win, Lang Lang. It's impossible."

Her words were like a knife through my heart. Didn't she think I had the talent, the focus, or the maturity?

"Why not?" I asked again.

"Your competition is too strong. Not just from Zhe and Yu, but there are eighteen-year-olds from around the world who have already won international competitions. Lang Lang, go to Germany with the idea that it's the experience that will be your reward."

Her words, while sincere, angered me. I suddenly wanted to practice the repertoire that Professor Zhao had chosen for me. I was determined to play Chopin and Liszt with perfection. I was determined to win. Whether it was Monkey King, a kung fu master, or simply my own work ethic, I knew I would find something to push me to the top.

We stayed in line at the embassy, as my father refused to leave. He brought up Yu and Zhe again, asking the official why they had gotten visas so quickly but we couldn't.

"They are officially representing your country," the German official replied. "Why isn't your son representing your country? If he were, I could overlook the health insurance issue."

"He is young and has already won many competitions," my father said, skirting the question.

"Sir, again, you have no job. We can't issue you a visa."

"My job is to make sure my son becomes the number one piano player in the world."

"That isn't a job. That's a wild dream."

"A dream you're destroying if you won't let us into Germany."

"Rules are rules," the man said stiffly.

By chance, a Chinese guard at the embassy overheard my father arguing with the bureaucrat, and recognized his accent as coming from a province in northeast China. It turned out the guard, who grew up in a city not far from Shenyang, had attended the middle school established by my father's grandfather, a well-known educator. The guard and my father quickly became buddies. After my father explained our frustration and our urgent need to get to Germany, the guard told us not to worry, that we should speak to a certain visa counselor, a lady who loved children and music. And help us she did. Twenty-four hours later, we both had our stamped passports and visas.

In the meantime, my father was beseeching every relative and friend he knew to loan us U.S. $5,000 to get to Germany. He finally raised $3,000 and had to beg for a bank loan to make up the difference. Zhe and Yu, because they had the backing of the government, had all their expenses covered.

The day we were to leave, my father and I were standing in line at passport control at Beijing's international airport. By coincidence, Zhe and Yu were directly in front of us. They didn't bother to turn around, and even if they had, I'm not sure they would have recognized me.

"Diplomatic passports!" the official exclaimed to Zhe and Yu. "You must be representing our country. In what capacity?"

"We're pianists, on our way to an important international piano competition," said Yu.

The official beamed. "Well, China is proud of you. I know you'll come back with high honors!"

When I marched up to the same official, I could barely see over his counter as I handed him my passport.

"Why are you going to Germany?" he asked.

"I'm going to enter the same piano competition."

"But you have only a normal passport."

"The government is paying for them. My family is paying for me."

"Does that mean you're not as good as they are?"

I was upset by his insinuation. I wondered what his other job besides passport control was—possibly music critic? My father stepped up and answered for me.

"His name is Lang Lang. Do not forget that name. He will be number one."

"Sounds like wishful thinking," said the official, and waved us through to the jetway.

It was my first time ever on a plane. As I walked down the aisle, I saw Zhe and Yu sitting in large comfortable seats. There were two seats just like theirs across the aisle, and I started to sit down. The flight attendant stopped me.

"Are you in first class?" she asked.

I had no idea what she meant.

"No, we are in economy," my father answered, showing our tickets.

Not only were we in economy, I soon learned, we were at the very back of the plane. The weather was often turbulent, pushing the plane up and down as if it were a glider at the mercy of the wind. I squeezed my eyes shut and grabbed my father's hand. Was all this another omen?

When we finally landed in Frankfurt, I watched as Zhe and Yu were welcomed by an official committee, who also whisked them through customs. I spent almost an hour getting cleared. My father's mood had turned gloomy, and I was sure I knew why. He had bet everything on my success in Germany—emotionally as well as financially—and if I failed, he would be in debt for a long time, maybe forever. As a citizen of China, his personal honor and reputation were at stake. Everything depended on me. I couldn't let him down.

On our first night, we stayed in a dormitory room on the outskirts of Frankfurt lent to us by a relative of one of Professor Zhao's students. My dad and I slept on the floor; Professor Zhao slept on the bed. I imagined Zhe and Yu were settled comfortably in a first-class hotel. I slept intermittently, bothered by jet lag, the hard floor, and a general sense of being overwhelmed.

In the morning, while my father slept, I explored the neighborhood. China was showing a few signs of

Western-like prosperity, but this *was* the West, a land of German luxury cars zipping around corners, the smell of fresh coffee and pastries wafting from stylish cafés, and blond-haired women and tall, handsome men in expensive clothes walking to work. As much as I might miss Shenyang, I knew at that moment I would need to leave my country, at least for a while.

That afternoon we took a train back to the center of Frankfurt. The next week we would take another train to Ettlingen, where the competition would be held, but first we had to find a hotel in Frankfurt, which would allow me some time to get over the jet lag before the competition started. I was sure my father was entertaining the idea of sleeping in the train station. With my unquenchable curiosity, I strolled ahead of my father and Professor Zhao through an affluent neighborhood, admiring the houses. Suddenly I saw a Chinese man. He was washing a large black sedan with a license plate that read "8888"—in China four eights means good fortune—in the driveway of an impressive-looking house. I wondered if he worked for the owner. Once we introduced ourselves, I was startled to learn that the car and house belonged to him. Mr. Huang and his family had moved permanently to Frankfurt and now owned three Chinese restaurants here.

I told him I played the piano and was entering a competition in Ettlingen in a week.

"You play the piano, really?" he asked. "My daughter is learning to play the piano!"

When my father and Professor Zhao caught up with

me, Mr. Huang invited us into his home and fixed us a tasty lunch of German food, and I played a Bach sonata for him. He was so impressed that he made us a deal. We could stay with him all week—room and board for free— if I would give his daughter a one-hour lesson every day. My father, Professor Zhao, and I were thrilled at the opportunity. For the next week I cheerfully carried out my obligation, and in my free time Professor Zhao and I had a piano at our disposal. Looking back on this week, I often wonder if I would have done so well in Ettlingen if not for the extended rest, good food, and plenty of practice. Maybe Monkey King and my kung fu master had me in their sights the whole time.

Once we reached Ettlingen, the contest sponsors gave every participant a separate rehearsal space. Wandering down the hallway, looking for a private room that hadn't been taken, I suddenly overheard the most magical notes coming through a half-open door. When my father and I peeked in, I saw the back of a young man, maybe sixteen or seventeen years old, and as he played he swayed back and forth in a free-form motion. I had never seen anything like it. When I played, my posture was as rigid as a two-by-four.

"He's blind," my father whispered to me.

Intrigued, I just watched. The boy seemed to sense our presence even before I walked over and sat on the bench beside him. The boy turned his head to me, and I saw that his eyes were squinted closed. My English was no better than his, but I found out that he was Japanese and his name was Akira. Akira didn't seem bothered by the fact that we both would be competing and asked if I would play something for him. I chose Liszt's "Tarantella," which I would perform in the competition. It's a highly charged piece, with a rapid tempo in 6/8 time, about a poisonous tarantula that bites women. If you're infected with its powerful, hallucinogenic poison, you must do a special dance to rid your body of the venom and to ward off death.

"Yes, yes, very good, very good," he praised me when I finished.

Then he played the same composition, except it was a very different interpretation. He played with far greater sensitivity, a softer, more delicate touch on the keys, and he never strained to capture the emotion. He *became* the emotion. The joy of the dance sprang from his heart, not his head. His sightless touch showed me how important feeling, as opposed to technical excellence, was in creating total musicality.

We played more songs for each other, not as competitors but to show our mutual love for music. I was amazed, stunned, and moved to be sitting next to him. At this point in my life, I had heard hundreds of pianists, but none like Akira. When I finally told him my age, he said, "I'm lucky you are in a younger group or else you would beat me." It was a two-tier competition: Group A included students age eleven to sixteen, and Group B included students ages seventeen to twenty.

"I'm the lucky one. You are unbeatable," I said in my

primitive English, which in turn made me aware of how primitive my interpretation of music was. At this most inconvenient time, just before the most important competition of my life, I was suddenly questioning how I played the piano.

The next morning, five minutes before the contest, I played "Tarantella" for Professor Zhao, but not the way he had taught me. Through Akira I had discovered the true spirit of the composition.

"My God, Lang Lang," Professor Zhao exclaimed. "There's a wrong note in there."

I'm sure he was right, but I was scarcely aware of which one it was. I was too wrapped up in the beauty of the overall composition. A nervous Professor Zhao said I had to redo the whole piece the way I had originally been taught it; otherwise, I was in danger of duplicating my mistake for the judges.

"I don't think I can do that," I said. "If I do, everything will fall apart."

As he thought about it, Professor Zhao agreed that, the wrong note aside, my sensitivity and touch had been superb. If I had the ability to correct my technical lapse but leave the interpretation in place, it would be an accomplishment the judges could not ignore.

Walking into the concert hall, my father and Professor Zhao took their seats, but not before I got the usual pat on the back from my father. When I marched onto the stage,

Me, Lang Lang, four months old.

As a kid, I loved uniforms, army caps, and toy pistols. *Top:* Having fun with my mother in our Shenyang air force base apartment (age three). *Bottom:* In front of the military airport next to the air force base (age three and a half).

It was fun to imitate Monkey King's kung fu moves (age five)!

I also really liked to draw (age five).

I enjoyed my lessons at Professor Zhu's home. I'm wearing a children's marine uniform (age five and a half).

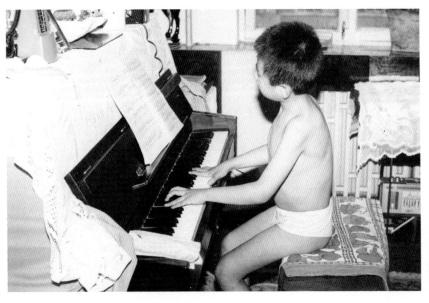

Even during the hot summer months, I practiced eight hours a day in our Shenyang home. We didn't even have a fan (age seven)!

In front of the Great Wall of China (age seven).

With Professor Zhao, after taking first prize at the Fifth Xinghai National Piano Competition. It was my first professional competition (age ten).

Practicing at home in Beijing. My bunk bed is on the left, along with my cousin Yi Feng's; my dad's bed is on the right (age twelve).

My mother (seated) listened to me practice when she visited us in Beijing.

Performing during the final round of the International Tchaikovsky Competition with the Moscow Philharmonic Orchestra in Japan (age thirteen).

With my father, after winning first prize.

I received warm applause when I played at Steinway Hall in New York City during my first visit to the U.S. in 1996 (age fourteen).

I got my big break at age seventeen in Chicago when I substituted for André Watts at the Ravinia Festival's Gala of the Century. My current mentor, Christoph Eschenbach, conducted the Chicago Symphony Orchestra.

Dean Gary Graffman was my teacher at the Curtis Institute of Music. *Top:* At a lesson with Graffman. *Bottom:* It was a proud day when I graduated from Curtis in 2002.

I belong to the Man ethnicity and dressed as a Qing Dynasty emperor (also a Man) upon my return trip to China in 2001. I returned as the guest pianist when the Philadelphia Orchestra gave a concert in Beijing's Great Hall of the People.

In 2003 I taught a master class to budding musicians in Detroit. I even mimicked Mozart at the piano for them.

A huge fan, I was thrilled to meet Jin Yong (pen name Louis Cha), superstar author of martial arts novels, when his work was honored in Hong Kong in 2005.

Taking a bow with conductor Zubin Mehta in Vienna in 2005. The open-air concert at the Schloss Schönbrunn was attended by more than 100,000 people.

At Berlin's Waldbühne in 2006 in front of an audience of 20,000, I played Beethoven's Piano Concerto no. 5. My teacher Daniel Barenboim conducted.

With conductor Sir Simon Rattle in 2006, after performing with the Berlin Philharmonic.

In 2007, for a documentary, I played a late-afternoon concert at the Great Wall of China.

That same year, I played the Yellow River Concerto at the Yellow River.

Crazy about Transformers since I was a child,
I was remembering the old days and couldn't put
this one down during a recent dinner.

In 2005 my parents and I enjoyed our first family holiday in years in Lucerne, Switzerland.

looking out at the audience, I felt humbled as I imagined Brahms conducting his own symphonies in this very hall. I was scheduled to play early in the competition, before Zhe and Yu, but my position didn't bother me as much as it had in my previous competitions. My inspiration now was at fever pitch. I would play the music my way, and let the chips fall where they might.

I started with a Haydn sonata, then followed with Chopin's black key études and a Chinese piece before my finale, "Tarantella." I thought I played Liszt as lyrically as had my Japanese mentor, as the composer himself intended the piece to be rendered. When I stood and took my bow, the concert hall exploded with thunderous applause, accompanied by a standing ovation. I was called back to take five separate bows, and when I finally left the stage, I had wings on my shoes.

Zhe's and Yu's performances were nothing short of brilliant. Their technical skills were superior to mine, yet I didn't squirm in my seat from anxiety or insecurity. I had played with such heart that I didn't think Zhe, Yu, or any of the other competitors—Russians, Spaniards, Italians, French, Germans, Austrians, and Americans—had come close to me. But I would be the first to admit that I was feeling a surge of adrenaline from being totally in love with the music I had just played. Objectivity was not my strong suit.

When it was time to announce the winners, our German host walked up to the microphone. He spoke in his native language, so I had to keep asking Professor

Zhao, who sat next to me, for a translation. My father was in the balcony behind us because there wasn't room for him below.

Pulling out a piece of paper, the host began with the consolation prizes, which went to a Ukrainian, a Lithuanian, and a Spaniard. Number five was the Chinese boy. He started crying because he was placed fifth.

Fourth place was awarded to a Russian boy. Third went to a girl from France.

The audience grew silent as he studied his list. I didn't want to be number two. Egotistically, perhaps, I saw this as a defeat. I clamped my hands over my ears because I feared hearing my name called.

"Number two is from China," Professor Zhao whispered to me, pulling my hands from my ears as he interpreted the host's next remark.

Oh no, I thought. It had to be me. Or worse, what if it was Yu, and Zhe was number one? I had been so caught up in my zeal, perhaps my ambition had overreached my talent. What if I had finished out of the running altogether? I thought of my father, the debt he had taken on, and the faith he had placed in my abilities.

"Number two," intoned our German host, "is Yu."

I stole a glance at Yu as the auditorium broke into polite applause. He looked furious. I knew that in his mind I was a runt, an upstart who deserved to be beaten. When the applause was replaced by a tomb-like silence, the only sound I heard was my runaway heart. My gaze immediately searched out Zhe. He looked calm and collected, as if he was certain of the outcome.

"As many of you know," the host added, "some years we have forgone a first prize altogether. There simply has not been the talent to justify it. But this is not one of those years. This year, in fact, is just the opposite. We are blessed to have a young pianist who towered above all the others."

I was fidgeting in my seat. My face had turned warm. And then I heard my name: "Lang Lang." I had in fact won the first prize. It felt as if I had won the World Cup—the striker who scores the championship-winning goal.

Two years later, I had the chance to see a video of the award ceremony, and there is a shot of my father in the balcony weeping for joy. I'd never seen my father crying. It was a deep emotional time for me. Although my father never showed it, he felt proud.

I reached over and hugged Professor Zhao. "But there is more," the host continued. "This year we are also awarding Lang Lang a special award for the most outstanding artistic performance in the history of our competition."

Two prizes! And one created just for me! I was dizzy with the thought that I had bested not just the highest-ranking young pianists in the world this year but even those from the past. I couldn't stop jumping up and down and letting out more than one scream.

After the applause had died down, a famous Chinese piano professor walked up to me. With great sincerity and kindness, he said, "Lang Lang, I've never heard anyone play as you played today. God was moving your fingers. God was whispering in your ear."

The words affected me profoundly, but I didn't think

of God as inspiring me so much as Akira, my Japanese friend, whom I found at the back of the auditorium, sitting by himself. I wrapped my arms around him.

"You played so well," Akira said, "beyond anyone's expectations . . . except mine. I knew you could do this. Congratulations, Lang Lang."

"Thank you, Akira. I'll never forget you."

And I never have.

{ 13 }

Upon our return to Beijing, my father and I had expected, if not the red carpet treatment, some public recognition of my achievement in Germany. Zhe and Yu had received a hero's farewell, but there was neither a camera crew, a government official, nor a teacher from the conservatory to greet or congratulate us.

"Don't worry," said my father, sensing my disappointment. "Our prize money will enable us to pay back our relatives and the bank and still have a little left over. Everyone who knows you is proud of you. But don't expect much from the conservatory. *Especially* the conservatory. It is a great institute of learning, but it's also a hotbed of jealousy. Be prepared."

I listened to my father's words, but I didn't understand. I was blinded by a twelve-year-old's ego. I wanted the attention and accolades I thought I had earned. A few months later, when I auditioned for the middle-school sector of the conservatory, I played brilliantly and assumed I would be ranked first in my class, particularly because the other students' performances were just average. The judges, as if to teach me my place, decided to make me third. Both Professor Angry and Professor Zhao had been part of the panel of judges.

I was bewildered. But it was my father, despite having warned me about envy and jealousy at the conservatory, who was the most agitated. He went up to the judges and began screaming.

"You have it in for Lang Lang! You know he's number one. He was number one in Ettlingen, winning first place over the best pianists in Europe, if not the world. If he could achieve that status, he can certainly do that here in the middle school! You gave him third place to humiliate him, to demonstrate how powerful you are. You push your own students so you can push your own careers and get your own bribes! It's outrageous!"

My father was beside himself. I was embarrassed as he raved, and for the charges he never should have made in public. He blamed Professor Zhao in particular for not having the courage to stand up to Professor Angry. Professor Zhao had been quick to take credit with the media for my success in Ettlingen, my father said, but he had turned silent in the conservatory, as if afraid of local politics.

There was no way to quench my father's rage. Turning his back on Professor Zhao, he soon courted the attention of another renowned piano teacher, Yin Chengzong. Unlike my father, Mr. Yin was a huge musical star during the Cultural Revolution. He was the musician who made the Yellow River Concerto famous. He had placed second at the famous Tchaikovsky competition in Moscow in 1962. He took on only the most promising students. A scholar of Russian music, he both spoke the language and had mastered the Russian approach to piano. When he heard me play Rachmaninoff and Tchaikovsky, he encouraged me to pursue those composers' most difficult pieces.

When Mr. Yin agreed to give me lessons, my father knew not to tell Professor Zhao. Chinese teachers didn't like sharing their star pupils. And despite his anger, my father knew Professor Zhao was still an influential ally. I began taking lessons with Mr. Yin in secret, even though it made me feel awkward.

When my mother came to visit us in Beijing, I told her about my sessions with Mr. Yin, and my father's ulterior motive for finding still more teachers for me.

"He wants to prepare me for another competition," I explained. "The International Tchaikovsky Competition. It takes place in Japan next summer."

"He's already told me, Lang Lang. And I support his decision. Do you?"

Despite my recent setback at the conservatory, or because of it, I was hungrier than ever for a competition that would prove my worth as a serious pianist. "Will you come with us to Japan, mother?"

"I'd love to, my darling. But if the Chinese government sponsors you—and I hope they will—they won't pay for more than two tickets. It's your father who must go with you, as always."

I hugged my mother tightly, accepting both the truth of her statement and the fact that she was very much part of our team—mother, father, and son—united in the great adventure to cultivate my talent. She had an ego too, but of the three of us hers was the most controlled, the most conditioned to sacrifice. As much as she missed me, she never complained. She would make any sacrifice for me. I wished I could return the favor. The only possible way was to continue to practice eight, ten, even twelve hours a day, connecting my heart to hers through music. I was in Beijing and she was in Shenyang, but I knew she could hear me playing every day.

When she took the train back to Shenyang, my father returned to his rote pep talks. By now I had them memorized; only the name and rules of the competition were changed. And the stakes. The Tchaikovsky contest was far more significant than Germany. The top six finalists would play with the Moscow Philharmonic. The top three would appear on international television. When I became number one in Japan, I would be recognized all over the world. I would win a scholarship to a school such as Juilliard or Curtis in the United States. My father was certain of it.

His words stoked my dream of not just visiting the West again but living and attending school there. In the next six months I practiced a nearly infinite number of hours, learning from both Professor Zhao and Mr. Yin. A conflict soon emerged. Professor Zhao thought I should play Mozart for the competition, while Mr. Yin insisted on Beethoven. I was far more comfortable with Beethoven than Mozart, whose genius I was just beginning to understand, but my father thought that Chopin's Concerto no. 2 would reveal my deepest skills to the judges.

However, still another teacher my father had asked to give me lessons, Professor Hu, who was as famous and highly regarded as Professor Zhao, chimed in with her strong opinion. Under no circumstances, she said, should I attempt Chopin's Concerto no. 2. It was about romantic love and the poetic stirrings of the soul, which I was simply too young to understand or convey musically.

My father shook his head as he and I left my practice session with Professor Hu. "Play the Chopin, Lang Lang," he said.

"Are you sure?"

"Teachers always underestimate you. Professor Hu is no different."

"But Chopin was a romantic and in love when he wrote some of his concertos. I've never been in love."

"He was longing for a lost love. Think about the love you feel for your mother when you play it. The feeling of missing her deep in your heart, put that into your music."

I knew what he was talking about. Perhaps the strategy would work. From my Japanese friend Akira I had already learned about the subtle but intricate marriage of feeling and technique; the Chopin concerto would ask me to explore my emotions even more deeply.

When my mother came to visit, a few months before we were to leave for Japan, I told her what I would be playing and why. She wrapped me in her arms, giving me back the same love I felt for her, and letting me know how successful I would be. Then she passed on less positive news. At Professor Zhao's insistence, she and my teacher had met privately. He had complained to her that my father was undermining my future by continually interfering with faculty and staff. He was alienating everyone, including Professor Zhao. He argued, he ranted, he raved. He had no manners and no judgment. And he was obsessed with my career.

"What did you say?" I asked, knowing that some of this was definitely true.

"I defended your father. I never claimed that he was perfect, only that nothing was more important to him, or me, than your talent. Professor Zhao said that because of your father's obsession, teachers at the conservatory resented both of you."

"But that's not fair," I said. "What they feel about

either of us should have nothing to do with how they feel about my piano skills."

"Your father spoke the truth when he said the conservatory is full of backbiters and hypocrites. Professor Zhao was really angry, I think, because your father doesn't want you to play Mozart. If you don't play Mozart, Professor Zhao insisted, you will never do well in Japan. He doesn't expect you to place higher than third, if that."

When my mother repeated this conversation to my father, he scoffed at Professor Zhao's prediction. "Don't believe anyone who says Lang Lang will not be number one."

But I was shaken. If Professor Zhao, who had arduously prepared me for the German competition and who had taken partial credit for my triumph, didn't think I could win in Japan, why should I?

With only two months before the Tchaikovsky contest, my mother made a bold suggestion. She knew my confidence was shaken, and she wanted me to return to Shenyang and take lessons from my first teacher, Professor Zhu. I thought my father would argue her down, but not this time. He saw the wisdom of making me as comfortable as possible before I left for Japan. Playing Chopin would be my greatest challenge yet, and Professor Zhu, in the end, knew me and my skills as well as anyone did. By agreeing with my mother, perhaps my father was also acknowledging his error in being confrontational with the faculty. This would be the closest he had ever come to admitting he had done something wrong.

*   *   *

The minute the train pulled into the Shenyang station, a wave of calm washed over me. I was alone with my mother, which made me extremely happy, and returning to my former apartment, which looked exactly as I remembered it, replenished my spirits. Along with my mother's incredible cooking!

Nothing had changed at Professor Zhu's apartment either—the same piano, the same pictures on the wall, the same patience and sympathy she had offered me from the day we first met. When I told her the controversy I'd created by choosing to perform Chopin's Concerto no. 2 for the Tchaikovsky competition, she asked me to play the piece, not once but twice. After the second time, she had tears in her eyes.

"As you know by now, Lang Lang, there are deep emotions in this piece, and you must play them with sincerity, without fear or embarrassment. If you can achieve that, and I know you can with practice, you will undoubtedly impress the judges. You are a twelve-year-old on the outside, but on the inside they will see the maturity and sensitivity of a much older artist.

"I have watched your career with great interest and seen how your age can work for you or against you. Sometimes being a prodigy provokes jealousy, but other times, as in Germany, being a kid definitely helped. Everyone wondered how someone so young could play with such extraordinary grace. Now, going to Japan, you'll be turning thirteen and tackling a piece as difficult as this concerto. People will note your age and think this is impossible. So you will have the opportunity, as you did in Germany, to show that your beautiful spirit and soul do not have an age. Your young body is but a shell for a wisdom beyond measure."

Except for my mother, no one could make me feel as good as Professor Zhu. The week before I left for Japan with my father and Professor Zhao, I played Chopin as perfectly as I could for my favorite teacher. It was a moment I wanted to hold on to forever, and if I could have packed that flawless performance in my suitcase and taken it out onstage in Japan, I could not have been happier.

Arriving in Tokyo on an August morning in 1995 was more jarring than traveling to Germany the year before. The language, the customs, and the bustling crowds of Japan's capital overwhelmed me. I was disoriented for days as we traveled to a city called Seidai, where hundreds of pianists from eighty countries, including ten pianists from China, would compete for the prestigious Tchaikovsky prize. When I spotted a Japanese newspaper with the photo of a girl my age beaming as she stood by her piano, Professor Zhao told me Yuko was the best young pianist in Japan. The media and public loved her. No doubt Yuko would win the Tchaikovsky competition, he said.

"Do you know what she'll be playing?" I asked, pushing away the sting of his words.

"I don't know, but it hardly matters. She's extremely talented. And the head of the judging committee is Japanese. What more can I say?"

I didn't understand what was happening with Professor Zhao. He had turned into a defeatist, or perhaps he was showing his true feelings for my father and me. I suddenly wished he hadn't come with us, and for the next few days I avoided him as much as possible. My father still believed I would win, but not without more preparation. He told me that a girl from Ukraine was another favorite, because she had placed second in the last competition four years ago. With a week left before the event, he wanted me to observe both girls as they practiced in the rehearsal hall, to study their techniques. When I did, I saw that they played powerfully and confidently, but in my heart I knew not to pay too close attention. It didn't matter how well they played; it was the emotional depth with which I interpreted Chopin that was more relevant.

From among thousands who'd sent in tapes, the judges had selected seventy-four. As the contest began, after a few days the seventy-four competitors were whittled down to forty. They included all ten from China, so I was sure everyone in the conservatory was cheering. After the second and most critical round, however, the field was reduced to six, and China was left with only one representative: me. My final competitors were two Russians, a girl from Great Britain, and the Japanese and Ukrainian favorites. These contestants were all under sixteen years of age. The first round is classical-period works such as those of Bach, Beethoven, and Mozart, plus études to show one's technique. The second round consists of Romantic-period works such as those by Liszt and Chopin, plus a contemporary music piece. These two rounds are solos.

The last round is a piano concerto with orchestra. Each of us would have the honor to play with the Moscow Philharmonic, which was exhilarating to imagine, but I had a nagging fear. In my life, I had never played with a full orchestra, or any orchestra, for that matter. To arrange such a practice session would have cost thousands of dollars. When my father asked Professor Zhao if he could somehow make arrangements for us, he said, "Not if you don't have the money."

"Think of your mother," my father urged me the day of the finals, as I was about to enter a large auditorium with seats for sixteen hundred people. "Think how you love her. How you miss her. Put your love and longing for her into the concerto."

Then he gave me my pat on the back and I found myself striding toward the stage. I was remarkably calm despite the sight of the sixty-person orchestra, all of them in tuxedos. As for me, I was wearing a white shirt with a black bow tie and black pants. My mom had bought such cheap pants, you could see the white lining through the thin material. To this day my mom still regrets she didn't have the money to buy better pants for me to wear.

I was assuming, hoping, that my playing would be heightened by such an illustrious orchestra, but I had no idea what it would actually be like. It was beyond my control. I grabbed a breath and told myself to focus on my mother and Chopin.

After I finished, I thought that my wish had come true. The way I had played for Professor Zhu in Shenyang was exactly how I had played today. Maybe I'd performed even better. It was impossible to be certain, however, what with so many distractions and other extraordinary players competing as well. When the last competitor finished, I sat in the audience with my father and Professor Zhao.

The spokesman for the Tchaikovsky competition began by thanking all the contestants and praising their talents, then got right down to business. As was customary, he announced the winners in reverse order.

Number six was the girl from England. Five was the girl from Ukraine. Four and three were the Russians.

A murmur spread through the audience. It was down to me and the Japanese girl, the media darling, the one whom Professor Zhao had predicted no one could top. But Professor Zhao had also forecast that I would place no higher than third. He had been wrong once; would he be wrong again?

"Number two," intoned the spokesman, "is . . ."

He paused dramatically. I felt some eyes on me, but mostly they seemed to be directed at the Japanese girl. She looked as nervous as I felt. The smile of invulnerability in the newspaper photo had vanished.

"Yuko."

All at once the exquisite tension that had held me in my seat was released in a deep gasp.

"And our gold medal for this year's Tchaikovsky International Competition for Young Musicians goes to Lang Lang."

I was shaking as I stood and waved to the crowd. My father stood too. The applause thundered around us, over us, and out the doors of the auditorium, as if leading us to our next destination.

"I knew you'd be number one," Professor Zhao said to me when things quieted. "I just knew it."

Neither my father nor I had much to say to him. Reporters gathered around outside, flashes popping in our eyes. I made a statement saying that I was honored, and I congratulated everyone in the competition for playing well.

"What happens next?" someone asked.

"I don't know," I said.

"What we do know," my father told me later, when we were alone, "is that after this great victory, Lang Lang, your life will never be the same."

{ 14 }

Whether my father knew exactly *how* my life would be different or whether he was simply making a generalization, two major changes happened almost immediately upon my return to Beijing. The first was that I received the recognition I had long been seeking. In addition to my mother, whom I hugged as if we'd been apart for years, the president of the conservatory greeted us at the airport. So did the media. I was suddenly not only the king of the conservatory but also the subject of a new newspaper article every week. At the Beijing Concert Hall, I played the complete Twenty-four Etudes by

Chopin. When critics raved, it felt like all of China heard them.

The second change centered on Professor Zhao. He was now very different from the mild-mannered, reserved gentleman I had first taken lessons from. My choice of playing Chopin's Concerto no. 2 for the Tchaikovsky had been *his* decision, he told everyone. In Germany, it was Professor Zhao, not me, who had won the special award. He had discovered and nurtured my talent from the beginning. Now he was busy planning my future.

I never had the nerve to correct my teacher in public, but I told my father it was as if he had become my lord and master, a dictator. I didn't like it.

At a Beijing television studio the next month, I was scheduled to perform with other top young pianists. For weeks I had practiced Liszt's Hungarian Rhapsody no. 6 until every note and nuance was familiar to me. However, at the last minute, Professor Zhao and his wife, Madame Zhao, who were also at the studio, elected to give the piece to Wang, a former competitor of mine as well as Madame Zhao's prize pupil. I was instructed to find something else to play.

"That's unacceptable," my father said. "And unfair."

"Who are you to make such statements?" Madame Zhao replied. "You are nothing but a parent. We are professors."

"You have given Wang the composition that you knew Lang Lang has prepared for. Why would you do that?"

"What we do and don't do is our professional business," she shot back. As they began to argue, she suddenly called for security to have my father removed from the studio.

I had finally had enough. "If my father goes," I said over the commotion, "I go. And what's more, if I don't get to play the piece I've prepared, I'll leave too."

Professor Zhao looked shocked that I had spoken up. He consulted with his wife and they reluctantly agreed I could play that piece, Hungarian Rhapsody no. 6.

I got my way that afternoon, but after the blowup, the rift with Professor Zhao was too deep to be healed. Weeks later, during an appointment at his conservatory office, we had an argument about whether I was mature enough to play Rachmaninoff's Piano Concerto no. 3, considered to be the most technically difficult piece in piano repertoire. Professor Zhao insisted I was not. Further, he demanded that my father and I follow school curriculum, just like any other student.

"I don't care about your school rules," my father asserted. "Lang Lang is different from other students."

"No, Lang Guoren, he will follow the school curriculum, *my* curriculum."

My father paused. I think he had been waiting for this opening for some time. "Perhaps in the past, Professor Zhao, but not in the future. We've been invited to New York by Yin Chengzong."

This was news to me. Mr. Yin was even more famous in China's piano circles—indeed, the world—than Professor Zhao, and was currently teaching in the United States.

"I forbid it," snapped Professor Zhao. "Lang Lang is my student, not Yin's."

"Lang Lang is my son, Professor Zhao, not yours."

As we left the office, I was afraid my father had permanently severed our ties to the conservatory. Professor Zhao, despite his strong and often wrong opinions, was still my teacher. My father seemed unfazed. He would tell me later that I had outgrown the conservatory, if not China. The whole world was now our stage, and we would start by traveling to America. We had no money for this, of course, but that hardly bothered a cunning dreamer like my father. He would find a way. Untold opportunities awaited me in the wealthiest country in the world, he insisted over dinner that night. I nodded silently, hoping that once again he would be proven right.

{ 15 }

I'll never forget my first visit to New York, flying over the canyon of Manhattan skyscrapers and spotting the Chrysler Building, the Empire State Building, and Central Park before we landed. From the air it was impossible to pick out Carnegie Hall, but once my father and I were settled in Mr. Yin's apartment on the Upper East Side, I wasted little time in walking up and down Seventh Avenue between Fifty-sixth and Fifty-seventh Streets. Carnegie Hall was neither as old nor as ornate as I had expected from photographs I'd seen, but it was dignified nonetheless, above all for its history of famous performances. Two men whom I idolized, Arthur Rubinstein and Vladimir Horowitz, had enshrined Carnegie Hall as a mecca for great pianists. Staring at the building and its marquee, I had the audacity to dream that one day I would be playing on this stage, hovering under the ghosts of Rubinstein and Horowitz.

Make it come true, I prayed to the gods, and to whatever other mystic and mythic powers might have influence over the course of human events. I was only fourteen but already a very superstitious young man. Maybe it all started with Monkey King and my belief in his supernatural gifts, or my father's pat on the back before I marched onstage, or the Chinese belief that certain colors, such as red, and numbers, such as 8888, brought power and good fortune. I was also an artist who knew that talent alone would never help me fully realize my dreams. Luck, timing, and connections were up to the gods.

I had an appointment that morning not far from Carnegie Hall, only a block away at Steinway Hall, itself an imposing piece of architecture. Inside was an immense rotunda decorated with oil paintings of every important figure in the history of piano, both composers and artists. Mr. Yin had arranged for me to play before a group of prominent critics and teachers, and as my father and I walked into the rotunda and introduced ourselves, I realized how limited my English was. I was embarrassed. This was something I would have to work on. I ambled up onstage and sat behind the piano, waiting a moment for my thoughts to crystallize.

I repeated the program I had last played in Beijing, Chopin's Twenty-four Etudes, of which I had every note memorized. Not many fourteen-year-olds, not many pianists of any age, could say that. One of my gifts from an early age was to learn and memorize whatever my father asked of me. By putting in so many hours of practice, repetition definitely helped my memory, but I could also, for example, remember what mistakes I was liable to make on which composition, and I rarely made them a second time. I remembered unfailingly how to interpret certain pieces, which chords to emphasize, when to be lighthearted or romantic or passionate. And as soon as I had memorized those subtle things, I knew when and how to change the overall interpretation, adding my own clarity, precision, and sensitivity—my own signature—to a piece.

Each artist's musical genius springs mysteriously from his soul, but it wouldn't be possible without first mastering and memorizing the basics. The magical connection between brain, heart, soul, and hands can never be totally explained, but in great pianists it is impossible to miss.

After finishing my one-hour-and-ten-minute program, I received congratulations from almost everyone in the audience. An exuberant Mr. Yin told my father that I had lived up to all expectations, that word of my talent would spread like a brushfire through America, and he expected scholarship offers to roll in at any moment. Enthused, we stayed in Manhattan for a month, meeting with various teachers and school administrators. Everyone flattered me, but no college came up with a hard offer.

"It'll take a bit more time," Mr. Yin assured us. "Please be patient."

Patience has always been my weakness. Our apartment was more than comfortable, as it was Mr. Yin's own place—which allowed me plenty of time for lessons with him. The more time that passed, however, the more frustrated I became. I loved walking the streets of New York and feeling the pulse and competitive drive of the city, but at the same time I felt left out.

Out of the blue one afternoon, my father received a telegram that made both our jaws drop. It wasn't the scholarship offer I wanted, but a positive surprise nonetheless. My fame in China was growing. The president of my country, along with the Minister of Culture, had invited me to be the featured soloist for the opening gala of the China National Symphony Orchestra's inaugural concert.

For the moment I had to put America and my school plans on hold, my father said. It wasn't wise to neglect the president of your country. Of course that was an understatement. This was an incredible honor. We booked tickets home immediately. Besides anticipating the thrill of playing with China's most renowned orchestra, I was homesick and wanted to see my mother.

On September 16, 1996, before an audience filled with

dignitaries in business, arts, and government, a fourteen-year-old sat behind a grand piano in his impeccably tailored tuxedo and played Beethoven's Choral Fantasy. After the concert, President Jiang greeted me warmly. "You are a brilliant boy," he said, "and you represent our nation admirably."

After this huge success, the president of the Central Conservatory urged my father to remain in China, assuring him that he would obtain excellent American or Russian teachers for me. But my father's vision was clear: One way or another we were going back to the United States to study.

Our big break came a week or two later when I was visiting my mother in Shenyang. I received a letter from Gary Graffman, the famed concert pianist who had been a child prodigy as well as a student of Vladimir Horowitz. He was also currently serving as president of the Curtis Institute in Philadelphia. Along with Juilliard in New York City, Curtis was considered one of the top music conservatories in the world. While admission to both schools was ferociously competitive, students accepted to Curtis were automatically given full-tuition scholarships. Mr. Graffman had seen a video of my performance with the Moscow Philharmonic, when I had played Chopin's Concerto no. 2, and was sufficiently impressed to ask me to audition for Curtis.

I couldn't wait to fly back to the United States, and I wanted to bring my mother with me. As expected, my father informed me that financially we were strapped, and it would be a struggle for even the two of us to manage abroad. But it was my mother's salary we were managing on, I pointed out. It didn't seem fair that she was always the one sacrificing. I wanted her to speak up, even to demand to come with me, but once again she deferred to my father's judgment.

"In no time at all, you'll be home to visit, Lang Lang," she whispered.

In no time at all, I thought, I'd be twenty, and my mother would have spent virtually half my life without me. The thought had to be as painful to her as it was to me.

"Look," I pointed out, "Father doesn't know any more English than you do."

"True, but a strong man will make certain you are well cared for."

"If I get into Curtis, I don't know when I'll be coming back."

"Time flies, my son. You'll be back to China soon enough."

By the time we secured our visas and left Beijing, it was late spring. Arriving in Philadelphia, I found that a storm had blanketed the Curtis campus—a series of lovingly restored historic mansions on Rittenhouse Square, in the heart of Philadelphia—with a pristine coat of snow. Students and faculty drifted from building to building. Sounds of instruments floated out of windows and seemed to hang in the bleached blue sky. The atmosphere felt very different from Manhattan. When I walked through some of the buildings, everywhere I looked were Oriental rugs, classical pieces of furniture, and ornate woodwork and wainscoting. I found the spaces warm and comfortable—like a womb, I thought, a place to be nurtured. This was unlike the huge classrooms at the Beijing conservatory.

Mr. Graffman said, *"Nihao,"* greeting my father and me in Mandarin. Mr. Graffman was fashionably dressed. He had visited every corner of China. His office was filled with exquisite Chinese sculpture, calligraphy, and paintings from ancient dynasties. If I felt any jitters, he put me completely at ease, not only with his office décor but in prepping me for my audition. As we talked about my audition and what I had chosen to play, he never used the words *judged* or *evaluated*. Mr. Graffman made it all seem like a Sunday social. He simply said that a number of faculty members would be present and eager to hear me play. They had all heard such great things about my talent.

"Who will be there?" I asked.

"Leon Fleisher, Claude Frank, Seymour Lipkin, and Peter Serkin."

I must have looked concerned because Mr. Graffman added immediately, "Your job, Lang Lang, is to relax and enjoy your music as much as those who will be hearing it. It will be a wonderful day for you."

That night my nerves returned and I asked my father to sleep with his arm around me. The names Mr.

Graffman had recited were all familiar to me—titans in their respective fields. My father didn't have to remind me that I had to play flawlessly. By now I had internalized his message. Getting into Curtis was arguably even more important than winning in Japan or Germany.

We arrived on schedule at the main building on campus but became confused over where the audition would be held. Our English was so primitive that whenever we asked for help, we didn't understand the answers. I kept looking at my watch. I did not want to keep Mr. Graffman and his illustrious faculty waiting. Fortunately, we met a Chinese opera student who gave me explicit directions in Chinese to the audition room. He introduced himself as Ge Qun Wang, but added proudly that his American friends called him GQ. My father started to follow me upstairs but was stopped by our new friend.

"I'm sorry, sir," GQ said, "but parents are not allowed to attend auditions."

It was a similar policy at the China conservatories—parents usually had to wait outside the campus gates—so my father wasn't terribly surprised. Fearing I was late, I hurried up the stairs, only to hear a patter of feet behind me. It was GQ.

"Your father asked me to come up and pat you on the back and tell you that you're number one."

I smiled. The pat rekindled my confidence and made me feel my father was right beside me. Entering the room, I bowed to the distinguished committee, adjusted the bench behind the piano, and played with total focus and exhilaration: Beethoven's Sonata in A flat, op. 110, and then my favorite, Chopin's Etude no. 2.

The next night, for the second round, I played Chopin's Ballade no. 4 and Bach's Preludes and Fugue. The judges were joking with me, but I didn't know it. They said I needed to play faster. I was ready to do so, but they laughed and said it wasn't necessary. Then Mr. Graffman informed me that of all the students who had auditioned for the fall term, it was his and the committee's opinion that indeed I was number one. His words made me blush with relief and joy. When I returned in September for the fall term, added Mr. Graffman, I could count on not only a full-tuition scholarship but also room, board, and living expenses.

My father was elated, giving me one of his rare smiles, when I delivered the good news. In fact, he could barely catch his breath. At first, I thought his labored breathing was simply due to excitement, but the next day, on our flight back to Beijing, his breathing grew increasingly short. Something was terribly wrong, so I asked the flight attendant to have the pilot radio ahead and have an ambulance waiting at the airport. I kept gazing at my father, making sure he was comfortable, but wondering what was happening. I couldn't remember him being sick a day in his life.

When the plane touched ground, we were the first ones off. My mother was waiting along with an ambulance, and we rode with my father to the hospital. The next few days were filled with tension and little sleep as my father underwent a series of blood tests and X-rays. What if this was cancer? I quietly asked my mother. What if my father died? What would happen to us, and to my career? Every night I cried myself to sleep. My mother kept assuring me that he was a strong man and he would survive, no matter how bad the news. She was as emotionally dependent on him as I was.

Finally, the doctors consulted with us. There were two large tumors in his throat—tumors that had been there for fourteen years! They were blocking the flow of air to his lungs, but miraculously they were not malignant. A surgeon removed them the next day, but my father was ordered to stay in the hospital to recuperate. For days he was not allowed visitors, not even us, for fear he would talk too much and damage his throat.

When I was finally allowed to see him, I promised I would come every day.

"I don't want you visiting," he whispered hoarsely. "I want you practicing."

I had to smile at his stubbornness. When he was finally released from the hospital, he wasn't supposed to talk for a month. At first his silence took getting used to, but then it was almost a relief not to have him bossing me around. Yet he wasn't really silent. Everywhere he went he carried a notepad. My father had lots of ideas about Curtis and what we could accomplish in America. One afternoon, he scribbled a message that caught my mother and me off guard.

Before we leave China, we should do something big, he wrote.

"What?" I said, out loud.

He thought for a second, then dashed out two words on his pad. *Farewell tour.*

{ 16 }

Before my father's voice returned in full, I received lots of notes from him about the farewell tour, most of them centered on a novel idea. Money had always been a problem for us, and I knew my father was tired of us living off my mother's salary and borrowing from friends and banks. He decided that I had acquired enough fame not only to pull off a farewell tour, but that in Shanghai, China's business center and most prosperous city, we would find a promoter who could sell tickets to my concert.

"So I'm going to become a professional?" I asked him. I'd just turned fifteen. "Isn't this a little premature?" I had nothing against dreaming big, but sometimes I thought my father's ambitions were unrealistic.

My father paid no attention to my uncertainty, just as he paid no attention to anyone who doubted my talents. He was convinced that Shanghai would be the ultimate test for me.

Unlike Beijing, in the north, where I was well known, my reputation in Shanghai, in the south, was less secure. Some people referred to me as the "prodigy from the north," but few had heard me play. When the promoter charged top prices for my recital, there was some resentment: who did I think I was? I kept hearing. Yet the tickets sold out. I was more than a little nervous. I had a lot to prove.

And I proved it. I played sonatas from Beethoven and Mozart, and of course my favorites, the études from Chopin and Liszt's Hungarian Rhapsody no. 6. It was an ambitious program, but I felt the gods were with me, and I played flawlessly. In the papers the next day, the reviews were glowing. I continued on my tour and performed in my home city, Shenyang, to the same high praise.

Yet under the joy was a certain sadness and conflict in my heart. As my departure for the United States grew closer, I knew I might be gone for years. I would be saying good-bye to the city of my birth and early childhood, as well as to my mother. In my last few weeks at home, I wanted to spend as many hours with her as possible. As usual, my dad chided her for wasting my valuable time, which needed to be spent on English lessons and on the piano, he said. At one point my parents got into a terrible argument in front of me, and my mother began to weep. As I consoled her, I felt my anger flaring at my father. I hated the way he browbeat her. I hated that he failed to understand my need for her tenderness and love. And how could he be so unaware of his wife's needs and feelings?

Going through customs at the Beijing airport, I held on to a Chinese good-luck coin a friend had given me. On the plane I sat next to my father, but my thoughts focused on my mother. One day I would prove to her that all her years of sacrifice were not in vain. I would become successful and famous and buy a large house, and she would come and live with us.

"When will we see Mom next?" I asked.

"I don't know."

"A year? Two? Three?"

"In America, you must buckle down and study hard, Lang Lang. That should be your primary concern, not your mother."

The plane raced down the runway and glided through a cloud bank into the bluest of skies, as if all were right with the world. But inside I felt quite differently.

At the Philadelphia airport, we were met by a driver from Curtis who ferried us to our new home, a seventh-floor apartment in the heart of the city. Compared to where we had lived in China, particularly the hovel in

Beijing, I thought I had struck gold. We had heat, air-conditioning, a bathroom, a kitchen, and a spacious bedroom! Most impressive was the Steinway B piano that greeted us in the center of the living room. I rubbed the keys as if this couldn't be happening. Now I knew how much Curtis and its faculty believed in me. I looked at my father. He thought he was dreaming too.

My scholarship included not only free tuition, room, and board but also free lessons with Mr. Graffman, who, with his lovely wife, Naomi, would frequently invite my dad and me for dinner in the weeks and months to come. His knowledge and love of Chinese culture and history were shared by Naomi, who peppered me with questions about my childhood, early piano competitions, and how I felt about Chinese music. She was genuinely curious and obviously cared about us. I felt special in their presence. I knew that whatever advice Mr. Graffman offered me in the future, either as my teacher or about adapting to America, I would take it to heart.

In addition to piano lessons, Curtis paid for a private tutor to help me with English. My language skills were primitive, but not as painful as my father's, who basically didn't want to learn a new language. Maybe he didn't think that was his job, or he didn't care about American culture except for the opportunities it could afford my career. Whenever possible he began to rely on the boy everyone called GQ, the opera student we had met on our first visit to Curtis, who spoke perfect English. At twenty-five, GQ was ten years my senior. As he spent more and more time at our apartment, he became like a big brother to me, showing me where to hang out in my limited free time. He also helped with other practical matters such as setting up a bank account for us. Yet I refused to depend on him for English. Just as I had learned every nuance about the piano, I promised myself I would learn every quirk and subtlety regarding the English language.

At the same time I started at Curtis, I was required to attend a public high school for regular academic courses. I was one of only a handful of Asians in a school of predominantly black and white students. I was still shy and found it hard to make friends or speak up in class, particularly with my poor English. To ease my frustration, I would lose myself in music whenever I returned to Curtis. Music had always been and always would be my private universe for fantasy, power and happiness. Whenever I played I felt invincible, just as I had as a little boy with Monkey King at my side. The music I created surged like a bottomless river through my soul.

If I struggled with my new language, school was otherwise a breeze. I did my nightly homework in less than an hour, yet the next day I was better prepared than almost anyone in my classes. This was my first culture shock. American public high school students, I thought, were so lazy and academically indifferent that they made Chinese kids look like hardworking geniuses. American kids preferred to party, listen to music, buy clothes, drive cool cars, and eat fast food. I didn't look down on anyone because, frankly, I liked the American lifestyle. I was particularly drawn to street music, which we didn't have in China. Rap was hypnotic and powerfully rhythmic. I liked the way rappers waved their hands and jerked their heads. I couldn't understand everything they were saying, but it empowered me with a growing sense of independence, just as it did for American kids.

My father wasted no time in attacking my Americanized attitude. I think my new feelings must have struck him as ironic. He had once been accused of decadent bourgeois values and was sent to a rice farm as punishment, and now he was witnessing firsthand what he considered *real* bourgeois decadence. To straighten me out, he insisted I practice more hours than ever. Then he would hover beside me, waiting for a mistake so he could yell or even throw his shoe at me. In China, your father's word is never questioned, his will never disobeyed. In America, the kids I was hanging with defied and disrespected their parents at almost every turn.

Even before I made new friends in school, my tolerance for my father's authoritarian ways had been ebbing.

"Life in America is so much easier for me."

"Don't get fancy ideas, Lang Lang. I'm still your father and I'm still in charge. It's okay to be happy here, but don't get too happy."

I kept my cool. "I haven't forgotten why we're here. Nothing is more important to me than my piano and my career," I said honestly.

He stood with his arms crossed, eyes narrowed, almost not believing me. To irritate him further, I changed the subject to rap and musical artists such as the Notorious B.I.G., Jay-Z, Snoop Doggy Dogg, and Puff Daddy. I explained how rappers spoke in rhyme, that theirs was a music of spontaneity, sensuality, and rebellion, and that I was as fascinated by them as I was by Michael Jordan or Tiger Woods. His face paled even if he didn't know all those names. I knew what my father was thinking: I was rebelling against him. I was forsaking the rich tradition of classical music and preferring street thugs to geniuses such as Mozart, Chopin, and Tchaikovsky. I was abandoning my Chinese roots for American pop culture. He was so fearful of the new world we now inhabited that it was going to keep him up at night with worry, thinking up new strategies to keep me in line.

"What hogwash your head is filled with," he snapped, trying out his own slang.

I didn't argue because there was no point. Nothing would change my father or his inflexible beliefs. While I was adapting to my new home, he was becoming a stranger in a strange land. He clung to GQ when he needed help in English, and to a few Chinese acquaintances he had made in Philadelphia. Otherwise he kept to himself or hung around campus, eavesdropping on my practice sessions. I was still the center of his universe, and my success at Curtis and winning more competitions in our new homeland would be his success. He would not rest, I honestly believed, until I fulfilled the statement he had first made to Professor Zhao years ago. For my father to be happy and fulfilled, I had to become the best pianist in the world.

{ 17 }

On a more realistic level, entering and winning competitions were the one solid bond, the one dream, my father and I still shared. It gave us hope and kept us together as a team. But one afternoon, after finishing my lesson with Mr. Graffman at Curtis, my teacher shocked me.

"Lang Lang, I was thinking about Chinese artistic culture," he said. "It is so highly competitive on every level. Everyone is ranked. Hierarchies are found in every discipline—dance, painting, and music. The competitive spirit has contributed to your own development, Lang Lang. No one can deny it. You are with us today because of your success in Japan. Had you not won the Tchaikovsky, I never would have known about you. So I am grateful for the competitive spirit of your country."

I nodded, appreciating the rigors of my own culture, and that the path to success in China was unambiguous: you had to beat out everyone else in every contest you entered.

Mr. Graffman smiled, as if knowing what I was thinking. "Yes, your competitive culture offers you many benefits, but not here, not in the United States. The rules are different. It is my firm belief that your days of participating in competitions are over."

"How is that possible?" I asked. I knew my father had been going over a list of upcoming competitions, certain that I could win all of them. Winning contests was the name of the game. The more I won, the more I wanted to win. As much as I respected Mr. Graffman and hung on his every word, I couldn't agree with him this time. I knew my father wouldn't agree either. And his instinct for what moves were best for my career had so far been uncannily accurate.

"I live for being number one," I said, unashamed of my ambition. "What's wrong with contests?"

"They give you a particular attitude. They direct your energy away from the process to the prize. And in my view, Lang Lang, it can't be about the prize. It must be about the process."

"Excuse me, Mr. Graffman. I don't mean to be disrespectful, but what I've seen in your country is no different than in China. Look at Michael Jordan or Tiger Woods. It's all about being number one in your specialty. They're number one because they beat everyone else."

"That may be true for sports, Lang Lang, but classical music is different. While some teachers at Curtis push their students to compete, I prefer mine to ban such an idea from their thoughts. This allows them to concentrate on other aspects of playing the piano."

"What aspects?"

"Spiritual."

I suddenly thought of the Japanese boy whom I'd met in Germany, and the lesson he had conveyed about expressing my emotions in my music. He had been right. Maybe acquiring an understanding of spirituality was the next step for me.

When I relayed my conversation with Mr. Graffman to my father that evening, however, he disagreed wholeheartedly. Forsake competitions? That was crazy. I had to have goals, quantifiable goals, or I would lose track of my progress. He immediately made an appointment with my teacher. We had to take a Greyhound bus to New York and meet Mr. Graffman in his beautiful apartment there. It was in a historic building that overlooked Carnegie Hall and it was filled, as was his office at Curtis, with beautiful Chinese antiques.

"Without piling up an impressive list of victories," my father told Mr. Graffman in Chinese as we all sat in his living room, "how can we be assured that Lang Lang will become known to the public? How do we know he'll ever make a good living? We have sacrificed everything toward that goal."

As my father spoke, I thought of those stressful years in Beijing, the freezing winters in our heatless apartment, riding through the rain on a beat-up bicycle to the conservatory, and scrounging for food. At times we had lived off the mercy of strangers. I never wanted to live that way again.

"Your son will make a fine living as long as he keeps growing as a pianist. But not through competitions. Not through distractions. I will set up Lang Lang with a premier booking agent for the most famous orchestras in the country. That's the first step in building his career."

"And will this agent succeed? When can he book Lang Lang with the top orchestras?"

"Not right away. At first your son will be on the substitution list."

"What does that mean?" I asked.

"It means that when someone famous cancels, the agent starts calling those on the substitute list."

"Will I be the number one substitute?"

Mr. Graffman offered me a sympathetic smile. "Honestly, I don't think that's likely, not right away. But with time you will work your way up the list. And that period of time is essential for your growth as an artist."

To make us feel better, Mr. Graffman gave examples of composers and pianists who had gotten their career break by being on a substitute list: Leonard Bernstein, André Watts, Glenn Gould . . . each had been notified on the spur of the moment to fill in for one celebrity or another. Mr. Graffman paused and looked me, not my father, in the eye.

"Lang Lang," he said, "I will keep giving you lessons. Your nurturing and development depend on subtle changes in your playing. You will learn to wrap your imagination around the complex playfulness of Mozart and the dark tragedies of Tchaikovsky. Your soul will enter theirs. That's what I mean by spirituality. Ultimately, the sublime works of the great composers were written to touch us in a way that no words or pictures can possibly achieve. You are a poet of the piano, Lang Lang, and as such you must communicate with the human heart and soul. Am I making sense?"

This time I paused, looking my teacher back in the eye. "I think so," I replied. "But I still want to be number one."

{ 18 }

Number one. I had been raised to think that way. You could take the boy out of China, but you couldn't take China out of the boy. However, that didn't mean I wasn't totally absorbed in my lessons at Curtis or in understanding the nuances of Mr. Graffman's teaching. I wasn't even sixteen, but I felt much older in my ability to grasp the spiritual and musical sensitivity that was essential to my growth.

On the streets of Philadelphia, however, my growth was shaped by other, wilder forces. The enormous landscape of American pop culture, from rap music to sports to movies and television, opened my eyes to the extremes of behavior and emotion. Compared to China, America was awash in expressions of individuality and creativity. Almost nothing was forbidden. China was about tradition.

I existed in, and benefited from, both worlds: my structured life in the solemn, wood-paneled practice rooms of Curtis, and my serendipitous life wandering the streets and shops of downtown Philadelphia. For example, what did the television drama *Sex and the City,* which I loved to watch, have to do with Mozart's piano concertos? On one level, absolutely nothing, but on another level, for someone who had grown up on *Tom and Jerry* and kung fu fantasies as he played the piano, both stimulated my imagination and emboldened me to think in daring ways.

"Where have you been?" my father shouted when I returned one night from a Philadelphia 76ers basketball game. He had known where I was, but that didn't dampen his frustration that had been building over the last few weeks. No one had called us about a concert gig since we'd signed on with an agency. Without entering competitions, with nothing to formally mark my progress except reports from Mr. Graffman, my father was convinced my skills would diminish unless I practiced longer every day.

"Go and practice right now," he ordered.

"I'm tired," I said. "Tomorrow."

"You should never have gone with your friend to the basketball game. You should have stayed home."

"I'm tired," I repeated, heading to the bedroom. I was number four on the substitute list at the agency, and tapes of my performances had been distributed to a number of orchestras, all of which, according to my agent, had been well received. Still, our phone hadn't rung with the news we wanted to hear.

"Tomorrow is Sunday. Tomorrow you will practice for nine hours," my father declared.

"Seven."

"No."

"Who are you to say no?"

"Who are you to tell me what to do?"

"When the phone call comes from your agent, you must be ready."

"I am ready."

"Go to your room!"

That's exactly what I wanted to do, only I wished I didn't have to share the room with my father. It was moments like this when I most missed my mother and her calming presence, her warm, understanding eyes, the chance to talk to her, and for her to reason with my father. He and I barely spoke the next day. My hours of practice dragged because my mind was on so many other things, including my father's need for control.

A week later, I was practicing at Curtis, surrounded by a couple of my Chinese friends. My father was there too. He often came to watch me play, more so now because he thought I was picking up "bad American habits." As everyone watched, I tackled the monstrously technical

"Islamey" by the nineteenth-century Russian composer Balakirev. It would be a difficult piece for someone twice my age, but this was just the kind of challenge I thrived on. I played it three times from start to finish, until my fingers and mind were exhausted.

"Again," my father said from a corner of the room. His voice pierced me like a knife. "You made some mistakes."

I did as I was told because I didn't want to make a scene. When I finished, he ordered me to play the piece again.

My whole body tightened. I glanced at my friends, who fidgeted from embarrassment. I poised my fingers over the keyboard.

When I finished, my father raised his voice. "More mistakes. Ten more times."

My eyes narrowed on him, as if we were mortal enemies instead of flesh and blood. I was afraid of the words that would come out of my mouth.

"Ten more times, Lang Lang. Now!"

My friends' eyes swam between the two of us. They wanted to see what I would do. I lost all control. I erupted like a volcano.

"You are crazy!" I yelled at him. "A crazy tyrant. A crazy storm trooper. I am tired of your orders! I don't need you anymore!"

I thought he would throw his shoe at me. Instead, a look came over my father that I had never before witnessed. Like a child who had never expected to be reprimanded, his eyes suddenly filled with sadness.

"I am leaving," he said in front of all of us.

"Leaving what?"

"I am leaving here. Leaving America. Leaving you. I am going back to China."

My friends were as stunned as I was as he swept dramatically out of the room. I felt terrible for humiliating him in public, but equally glad that he would finally be out of my life. Part of me also didn't believe that he would carry out his threat.

The next morning, my father and I barely spoke as I watched him pack his bags and call a taxi. The next thing I knew he was gone. Left alone in our apartment, I felt a wave of anxiety wash over me. As angry as I could be at my father, I began to wonder how I could live without him. We had virtually never been apart. I remembered how nervous I had been when the doctors had discovered the pair of tumors in his throat.

I called my friends and we all rushed to the airport. We found my father in line, buying his ticket.

"This is crazy, Dad," I said. "Don't leave."

"You said you don't need me anymore," he answered.

"I'm sorry."

"Then you want me to stay?"

I told him I did. My clever father glanced around proudly, as if to announce to my friends he was still in control, or maybe that he had taught me a lesson. Father-son relationships are complex balancing acts, especially in our case.

{ 19 }

One thing I definitely needed to improve was my English. After I took a piano lesson with Mr. Graffman in his Manhattan apartment one morning, his wife, Naomi, served me tea and quickly became my confidante.

"I'm learning at my high school," I told her, "but I'd learn a lot more if my English were better. Particularly my comprehension. I'm taking private lessons, but they're not enough."

"You're such a positive person, Lang Lang. And you're not afraid of extra work. I think I know someone who can challenge you."

I loved the word "challenge." My ears immediately perked up. "Who?" I asked.

"His name is Dick Doran. He was an English professor at the University of Pennsylvania. He's retired from teaching but still holds a seat on the board at Curtis. He's the number two school administrator. I know you only like to hear about number one," she teased, "but he's also not a bad pianist and has always taken an interest in foreign students."

"Number two is fine," I replied, eager to hook up with anyone Naomi Graffman might recommend. She was an especially intelligent woman whose cultural interests were as deep as her connections to important and talented people.

I met Mr. Doran a few days later, at Curtis, and he quickly made an impression. He was of average height with dark hair.

"How do you do, Mr. Doran?"

"Call me Dick," he insisted. "And tell me how I can help you. Naomi said you wanted to be challenged."

"Okay, Dick. I need to know more about America than I'm learning in high school—culture, history, politics— and I need to improve my English at the same time."

"A noble aim. I can't deny you've come to the right man," he said with mock self-importance. "I believe Naomi told you I'm an old and very retired English professor. What do you know about Shakespeare?"

I blushed from ignorance. "Very little."

"We call him 'the Bard.' The greatest playwright in the

English language. There's relatively easy Shakespeare and difficult Shakespeare. With which would you prefer to start?"

"The harder the better," I said. "That's how I've always felt about music. If I can first learn the most complicated pieces by Rachmaninoff and Tchaikovsky, I know the rest will be easy."

"So it won't bother you to start with *Hamlet*? I'd say that was Mr. William Shakespeare at his very best. You'd certainly be challenged. Good grief, it challenges *me*!"

"I can't wait," I said honestly.

"We'll make a well-rounded young man out of you. Before you realize it, you'll be more American than most Americans."

My lessons started at a deliberately slow pace, with me reading out loud a few lines from act one of *Hamlet* and Dick explaining their meaning. He encouraged me to ask questions. It wasn't easy digesting Shakespeare's longest and most difficult play, but over the weeks I improved both my pronunciation—reciting Elizabethan English was almost like learning another language—and my comprehension. I was amazed by how much the English language had changed from the sixteenth to the twentieth century, particularly the slang I had fallen in love with on the streets.

Reading *Hamlet* offered lessons in psychology as well, and made me think of my relationship with my father. Hamlet, the melancholy prince of Denmark, was a sincere but conflicted character who knew his actions were sometimes wrong, yet he couldn't help himself. His emotions got in the way of reason. People he loved, such as Ophelia, he inadvertently ended up hurting. I was fascinated by his complexity, and quickly saw that Shakespeare, who wrote in iambic pentameter, was equally complex. How an author tells his story is as important as the story itself, Dick explained to me. The Bard's verses were a kind of music that required a special ear, I decided, and they reminded me of the melodies, counterpoints, and harmonies in the compositions I played.

I liked Dick for his warmth and patience. For all the biased and unfair teachers I had endured over the years, I had been blessed with extraordinary ones as well, from Professor Zhu and Mrs. Feng to Gary Graffman and Dick Doran. I always learn the most from those who show me kindness and patience, as if I need that to offset my own impatience.

Not only did Dick help me with English, he enlarged my cultural world by taking me to pop concerts and shows like *The Lion King*. For serious culture, I attended a performance by Luciano Pavarotti, the great Italian tenor, singing arias from Puccini and Verdi. His haunting, lyrical voice stayed with me for days, and he quickly became another of my musical heroes. Then there was George Gershwin, another of Dick's favorites and soon one of mine. George wrote the score and his older brother, Ira, penned the lyrics of their musicals. When I heard *Porgy and Bess* and "Rhapsody in Blue" onstage, blending classical composition with African American jazz, I understood the Gershwin genius.

Like a scroll unrolling before me day by day, I learned from the depth of Dick's interests and knowledge. There was almost nothing he didn't seem to be an expert on—culture, politics, war, government, race, capitalism—and I wanted to be an expert as well. At Curtis, I began to hang around American students, confident that I could meet their expectations not just musically but socially.

By the end of my second year in Philadelphia, I was satisfied with my growth as a pianist and my ability to fit in. I wanted to be accepted, trusted, and liked by everyone. One goal still eluded me, however. It was what made my father's behavior unpredictable on a daily basis: my agent hadn't called with a single offer for me to substitute. He kept telling me that while I was talented, I was too young to appear on the radar of major orchestras. Conductors had doubts that I had the soul to play Brahms or Liszt.

My father's only doubts were about my agent. Had we signed on with the right management team? I was equally frustrated, and when my father brought up the idea of entering competitions again, I couldn't disagree. He suggested I go to the Curtis library and copy down names of upcoming contests and the entrance requirements. I hurried over to campus and settled in a corner of the library. As I scribbled away, my eyes lifted to encounter a familiar face.

"Hello, Lang Lang," Naomi said. "What are you working on so diligently?"

"I'm researching," I replied, trying to think quickly.

"Researching what?"

I took a breath, fidgeting in my chair. I felt trapped. Should I lie? I didn't want to seem ungrateful to her husband for the advice he'd given my father and me. I didn't want to let down the two people who believed in me so deeply.

"I'm researching piano competitions," I admitted.

"Piano competitions? For you?"

"Yes."

"I must say I'm surprised, Lang Lang. Gary told you he thinks you're far beyond the contest stage. You're ready for the concert stage. You disagree?"

"It isn't that I disagree. I'm just frustrated. I like winning. Right now, nothing is happening for me."

"We all like winning. But if winning a contest keeps you from a bigger victory, we haven't won at all."

"What bigger victory?"

"An international career that satisfies you for the rest of your life."

Her words and faith in me were reassuring and put my goals back into perspective. She could have scolded me and I would have deserved it. But she wasn't mad or even disappointed. Like my mother, Naomi Graffman would always be understanding and nurturing, even when I got off track. After we said good-bye, I tore up my list of contests and walked back to our apartment. I told my father what had happened.

"All right," he said, respecting the Graffmans as much as I did. "We'll go along with your teacher. But something has to happen in your career, Lang Lang, and soon."

{20}

It wasn't soon enough, neither for my father nor me.

My life in Philadelphia had taken on a pattern—school, homework, some free time on weekends, piano lessons, and practice, lots of practice. I was playing some concertos so often that I had them committed to memory. That meant I could play for hours without a single sheet of music in front of me. Mr. Graffman didn't really comment on my feats of memory, as if he had expected this as part of my growth. He would occasionally give me some technical advice, but mostly he just watched and waited.

In my mind, I was already the pianist who was going to combine the sweetness of Rubinstein with the delicacy of Horowitz. Rubinstein was the ultimate musician, Horowitz the ultimate pianist. For me to accomplish that marriage would be a spiritual transformation. Every time I played I thought of the two men. I have always needed heroes in my life to inspire me: first I seek to emulate them, and then I try to equal them. Perhaps it was just my arrogance or naiveté pushing me, but without a grand dream I was afraid of wilting like a flower.

Every month my mother would write and occasionally call, asking how I was. *Lonely for you,* I wanted to say, but I was in my mid-teens and afraid of sounding like a little boy. I pretended everything was fine, including my relationship with my father. Secretly, I was tempted to get on a plane, as my father had threatened to do, and take my career back to China. I had now been away almost three years, and I worried the critics back home wouldn't even remember who I was.

In the fall of 1998 I finally got my first opportunity to substitute, but it didn't quite match the scale of my dreams. My agent arranged for a gig in New Mexico with an orchestra I had never heard of. Still, I was grateful to perform before a live audience, even if the orchestra sometimes played out of tune. In the spring of 1999 I had a second gig, in a small town in Pennsylvania. The crowd was pint-sized and my pay even more paltry. It was hard not to feel disappointed with my fledgling career.

My agent, however, told me not to fret. A bigger orchestra, in Knoxville, Tennessee, was ready to sign a contract with me. I was excited until I received word that the conductor had changed his mind. After an initial promise, an orchestra in Milwaukee backed out as well. I was number five for the substitute list for Cincinnati. Finally, the Houston Symphony came through, but it was in the middle of July in Houston in an outdoor venue. The air-conditioning onstage blew so unevenly that my left hand froze while my right hand sweated uncontrollably. The keys glistened with humidity. My fingers slipped. Every few minutes I heard a baby scream from the front row.

I was happy to leave Houston. My father and I began to wonder what had happened to the American dream that I had learned about from Dick. Maybe it didn't include substitute pianists. Frustrated, my father made almost daily calls to my agent, who responded with words I had heard before and learned to hate: "Lang Lang is young. Be patient. Don't call us, we'll call you."

One warm afternoon in the fall of 1998, my agent did call. "Good news, Lang Lang," he said.

"What?" I was afraid he would tell me of an engagement in a city I'd never heard of.

"Baltimore just phoned."

"The Baltimore Symphony?" I moved to the edge of my seat. This *was* big news. The Baltimore Symphony had just won a Grammy for a record made with Yo-Yo Ma, the famous cellist who had been born in Paris of Chinese parents, both of whom were musicians. Yo-Yo Ma was another of my heroes.

"When?" I said, barely able to breathe.

"The Baltimore Symphony will call you to set a date and discuss a repertoire. Are you ready?"

"I've been ready a long time."

"Well, good luck."

Within the month, I appeared with the Baltimore Symphony and played Beethoven's Choral Fantasy with the conductor Alan Gilbert to a standing ovation and positive media reviews. I was walking on air. This was the first time I felt the American audience's passion for me.

"This is it," my father, equally exuberant, said after my performance. "You're headed to the big time now."

My dream was to play with the Chicago Symphony Orchestra, whose brilliant music director was Maestro Daniel Barenboim, or to play at the Symphony's summer home at the Ravinia Festival in Highland Park, whose great conductor was Maestro Christoph Eschenbach.

But was I dreaming again? Worse, maybe I was delusional. Back from Baltimore, I called my agent and insisted he be in touch with Mr. Eschenbach. I was ready for the Chicago Symphony Orchestra, I announced proudly.

"The Chicago Symphony Orchestra?" he repeated, as if I had mentioned a place on the moon. "Are you kidding? That'll take you ten years."

"Ten years for what?"

"Ten years before they'll think seriously about you."

I dropped into stunned silence.

"You just don't get invited to play with Chicago or New York because you had a successful appearance in Baltimore. Be patient, Lang Lang."

Patience was one thing, ten years of patience was another. There was no way I could wait a whole decade. My agent, however, didn't have all bad news. He had an audition invitation from the Cleveland Orchestra. The orchestra was performing at Carnegie Hall for a few days, and if I could get to New York right away, this couldn't hurt my career.

After my father and I reached Carnegie Hall and met the conductor, I marched confidently up onto the stage, feeling the spirits of my two favorite ghosts, Horowitz and Rubinstein. The audition was grueling, but I thought I played well, exceptionally so. The conductor seemed pleased. I was sure Cleveland would be in touch with me.

My euphoria was short-lived. By now my father was running so low on funds that he insisted we take a bus back to Philadelphia, one without air-conditioning that ran out of Chinatown for $5 a person. I sank into my seat, and gradually almost into a depression. I wanted action, gigs, recognition and good fees. What if Cleveland didn't come through? What if I really did have to wait ten years? How were we going to survive? Would I be better off in Asia or Europe?

I believed in signs, omens, numbers, anything that would show me my future, but the only thing I felt truly lucky about that summer was my seventeenth birthday. I felt more confident than ever about my talents, and maybe, I thought, I was old enough finally to catch the attention of a major orchestra.

One afternoon, after practicing in our apartment all day, I wandered with my father into a local bookstore and rifled through the magazine rack. *Gramophone* and *BBC Music Magazine,* the two most important periodicals in my field, both carried features on the upcoming "Gala of the Century" at Ravinia. Christoph Eschenbach, the music director, and Zarin Mehta, the executive director of Ravinia and brother of Zubin Mehta, were planning a lavish show. Isaac Stern would be there, along with pianists André Watts. Leon Fleisher, and Alicia de Larrocha.

"This is where you should be playing," my father declared, looking over my shoulder at the article.

"Chicago doesn't want me, remember?"

We went home and ate leftover chicken. Maybe eating chicken is a good thing, a lucky thing, because an hour later I received an unexpected phone call from my agent. He had gotten a call from a stranger, a woman who had heard me audition at Carnegie Hall for the Cleveland Orchestra. A friend of Christoph Eschenbach, she had told him how talented I was. He was intrigued enough to offer me a twenty-minute audition if I could get to Ravinia by the end of the week.

"Can you make it?" my agent asked.

"I think so," I whispered, which was the understatement of the year. I glanced at my anxious father, who had eavesdropped on the conversation. We would have to buy plane tickets, using almost the rest of our savings, but this kind of opportunity wasn't just serendipity; it had to have come from the gods.

{ 21 }

We bought the cheapest air tickets we could and took a
taxi from the airport to get us to Highland Park, the
Chicago suburb that was home to the world-famous
Ravinia Festival. Ravinia, which had started as an amuse-
ment park in 1904, was the oldest outdoor music festival
in North America. Every summer, more than 600,000 fans
were treated to 150 programs that featured every genre
from bluegrass and folk to jazz and classical. For decades
it had been the summer home of the wildly popular
Chicago Symphony Orchestra.

My audition was scheduled not for the massive

outdoor pavilion but in a nearby smaller recital hall called the Martin Theater. When I walked in, I was greeted by a man who looked uncannily like Yul Brynner in *The King and I*. He was short, somewhat stocky, and completely bald, a rather intimidating figure. I recognized him from photos as Christoph Eschenbach.

"Maestro," I began, "I want to say how much I admire you, both as a conductor and as a pianist."

"Thank you. What are you going to play for me today, Lang Lang? We have just twenty minutes."

My heart was throbbing, but not from anxiety or intimidation. I felt only anticipation and joy. "I have a Haydn, a Brahms, a Rachmaninoff, and a Mozart. Your choice, Maestro."

I had given him a smorgasbord of the great composers, and I would be comfortable with whatever he selected. I knew my pieces by heart.

"Let's do Haydn," he said, sitting in a chair facing the piano.

I played a Haydn E-major sonata. I felt as if I did it faultlessly, but Mr. Eschenbach remained expressionless.

"Fine," he said. "Now Brahms, please."

I couldn't tell if he was in a hurry to get through the audition or if he was actually enjoying my music. "I have Brahms' Intermezzi. Do you have time, Maestro?"

"Please play it."

"What else?" he inquired when I'd finished the Intermezzi.

"Rachmaninoff Sonata no. 2."

"Ah, the Romantic one. Please play it."

My fingers glided over the keys with every romantic impulse I could command.

By now the twenty minutes had stretched to half an hour.

"Do you have Scriabin?" he inquired.

I hesitated. Alexander Scriabin, the late-nineteenth-century Russian composer and pianist, was known for lyrical and idiosyncratic atonal compositions. They weren't easy to play, but my father had made me practice them until my fingers throbbed. I knew his études from memory.

"Yes, I have Scriabin's études," I answered, and played through them without a hitch.

"What can you do with Mozart?" he asked next.

I offered a couple of concertos, then segued to Beethoven's sonatas.

"My goodness," Mr. Eschenbach suddenly exclaimed, glancing at his watch, "I've been here nearly two hours." He beamed at me. "You made me miss my rehearsal, young man!"

Minutes later, when Zarin Mehta, Ravinia's executive director, joined us, I was asked to play Schumann, Chopin, and Liszt.

"How many concertos do you have?" Mr. Mehta inquired when I'd finished.

"I know thirty. Twenty are completely memorized." I rattled off major ones by Tchaikovsky, Rachmaninoff, Prokofiev, and Beethoven.

"If you had a choice, which would you play as your debut with the Chicago Symphony Orchestra?"

For a moment I lost my voice, and I wasn't sure if I still had my mind. Was this an actual offer or just a hypothetical suggestion? The silence weighed on the whole room. I knew I couldn't keep Mr. Mehta waiting. I almost said Rachmaninoff's Piano Concerto no. 3, but at the last moment what tripped off my tongue was Tchaikovsky's Piano Concerto no. 1. I suddenly remembered how many careers had been galvanized by that brilliant composition—Horowitz's and Rubinstein's among them.

"A fine choice," Mr. Mehta said. "Thank you for your time, Lang Lang. You will be hearing from us."

On the plane back to Philadelphia my father said, "By fall, you will be concertizing with Chicago. You will be playing with one of the top five."

I didn't quite have my father's confidence. I had been burned too often in the past to get my hopes up. That night, in my dreams, I was flying over Lake Michigan, then the famous skyscrapers of downtown Chicago—the Sears building, the John Hancock Center and the famous sculpture by Picasso. My piano was my airplane. First it was a simple prop plane, then a small jet, then a jumbo, and finally a rocket ship spiraling at breakneck speed around the globe.

My bedside phone brought me back to consciousness. I looked at my watch: eight o'clock. I fought back a yawn and picked up the receiver.

"Are you awake, Lang Lang?" my agent asked cheerily.

"Barely." Everyone knew I was a late sleeper.

"Well, wake up. André Watts is due to play Ravinia tonight."

"So?"

"So he just called Zarin Mehta. He's too sick to perform. Mehta needs a replacement." For the first time I heard my agent's voice tremble with excitement. "They want you, Lang Lang."

"Me?" I was now fully awake but about to lapse into shock. I nudged my father in the next bed.

"You're going to play with the Chicago Symphony Orchestra in front of thirty thousand people and this is the 'Gala of the Century,' " my agent continued. "The concert is completely sold out."

"Tonight?"

"Tonight! Christoph wants the Tchaikovsky no. 1. You need to be at the Philadelphia airport in ninety minutes. A car will pick you and your father up in twenty."

My father was not only awake, he was up and running to the closet, picking out his only suit for the special occasion. "This is it, Lang Lang!" he proclaimed. "This is it!"

I still wasn't sure if "it" was a reality or a dream, whether I was still on my rocket ship hurtling through space or about to run downstairs to catch a car to the airport.

"Hurry," my father kept saying, as if the offer might be withdrawn at any moment until we showed up. "No time to lose."

As we flew to Chicago, I tried to settle my nerves and concentrate on Tchaikovsky. If this was going to be my biggest moment in a life of big moments, I couldn't afford a single lapse. I couldn't choke. I had always risen to the occasion, so why should this be any different? But my nerves were unusually on edge and I kept looking out the window, distracted by a hundred different thoughts. I wished my mother were here, and Professor Zhu, Uncle Number Two, and a half dozen other supporters. But they weren't. I was all alone.

Another car was waiting at O'Hare, and the driver whisked us to Highland Park and the grassy, tree-lined setting of Ravinia. As I approached the stage, the entire Chicago Symphony Orchestra, more than one hundred musicians, were tuning their instruments, as if waiting just for me. Standing next to Maestro Eschenbach was Isaac Stern, the legendary violinist and chairman of Carnegie Hall, who had once toured China and made a famous video, *From Mao to Mozart.* Then I glimpsed Alicia de Larrocha, the most renowned pianist in Spain, a woman of extraordinary talent whom I had long admired.

"We've heard so much about you, Lang Lang," she said warmly, approaching and shaking my hand. "We all want to hear your rehearsal."

They had come to hear *me*? I was floating on air as I nestled behind the piano and began playing Tchaikovsky with one of the greatest orchestras in the world. My nerves settled, even though my father hadn't had time to pat me on the back; I didn't need it this time. I was so filled with joy—with the music I was playing, with gratitude for those who had supported me all these years, and for the gods of chance that had placed me here—that I could have kept playing for hours.

"It's as though we've all been rehearsing for weeks," the maestro said when I'd finished.

In the evening, I put on my tux and stole a peek out my dressing room door. There, on the rolling, hilly lawn beyond the stage, were twenty-five thousand people of all ages, many gathered with picnic baskets and blankets. A tent, closer to the stage, held another five thousand fans. The weather was perfect, not too hot or humid, with a balmy breeze rippling through the night under a luminous moon.

When the featured artists had all finished and it was my turn, Isaac Stern announced to the crowd that André Watts was ill and couldn't perform, but a seventeen-year-old prodigy from China would give them a performance they'd be talking about for years. The applause welcomed me with an openness that only inspired me to live up to Isaac Stern's introduction.

I wondered if this was how Rubinstein and Horowitz had begun their careers, with a sense of destiny underscored by humility. Any pianist owes much of his success to the composers who understood the genius of the instrument for which they wrote. There is nothing like the piano to convey emotion, intellect, and—as Mr. Graffman taught me—spirituality. I played for almost half an hour, but it felt both longer and shorter, as if it were a dream. It felt timeless. It felt as if I were on a rocket ship and it was never going to land.

When I struck the last note, there was a brief silence, followed by a jolt of an explosion. "An electric charge," a critic would write the next day in the media. Thirty thousand people were suddenly on their feet shouting, "Bravo! Bravo! Bravo!"

When the evening was over and the crowd dispersed, Mr. Mehta and Mr. Eschenbach met me in the dressing room. The maestro had expected me to play well, he said, but not at this level. This was one of the greatest evenings in the history of Ravinia, he enthused, and then he asked if I wouldn't mind playing something else for them.

I didn't understand. The performance was over. It was nearly two in the morning. My father was waiting for me. "You mean tonight? Play for whom?"

"Yes, tonight indeed," he said. "Tonight Zarin and I, and all the featured artists, who are waiting outside, would love to hear you play Bach's Goldberg Variations."

"I don't have the score," I pointed out.

"You've memorized virtually every other famous piece; surely you know the Variations."

"But where will I play it?" I could feel my nerves coming back. This was not something I'd anticipated.

"We'll open up the Martin Theater next door. You'll give us a private recital."

"Of course," I said. "This is a rare honor." I had thought

that the evening was over, but in one sense it was just beginning.

I could feel their unbridled confidence in me, which matched the pressure I felt to succeed. I couldn't let them down. I suddenly realized the historical importance of this moment. When André Watts was sixteen, he'd substituted for Glenn Gould. Now the maestro and Mr. Mehta wanted the tradition to continue, as if it would bring good luck to everyone. I sensed this would also be my initiation into the world of classical music at its highest level.

I excused myself for a minute and found my father. "Are you sure you know the piece?" he asked after I explained what was happening.

"No, I'm not sure, not at all." I hadn't played the Goldberg Variations in two years. At this late hour, as I was still riding a wave of adrenaline, how could I be sure of my memory?

"What are you going to do?" he asked.

"I can't tell Christoph Eschenbach and Zarin Mehta no."

My father gave me a pat on the back. "Don't worry. You'll remember every note."

Back in the Martin Theater, when the lights were on and my audience comfortably settled, I adjusted the piano bench and positioned my fingers on the keys. I was afraid to look out at anyone for fear of losing my concentration. The legend behind the Variations was that Bach wrote it for Johann Gottlieb Goldberg because his friend couldn't fall asleep. In a sense, it was a long lullaby, and in another, the perfect and soothing end to the most unex-pected and astonishing day of my life.

As my father predicted, I did remember every note. It was four o'clock before we all said good night to each other, the cool air filled with talk of my future engage-ments with the Chicago Symphony Orchestra.

{22}

The news of my Ravinia debut circulated quickly around the classical music world and in the media. Reviewers said, "The seventeen-year-old stole the show. A major star is born!"

"I heard it was a lovefest," said Mr. Graffman a week later, when I was back to my more humble routine in Philadelphia. Ironically, he had been traveling in China while I was playing at Ravinia.

"I loved it, that's for sure."

"Wish I'd been there, Lang Lang."

"Me too. I owe a lot of my success to you."

"What for? You're the one with the talent and the work ethic."

"But you taught me patience, and to give up on the vanity of winning contests."

"That was hard for you, wasn't it? Naomi told me about finding you in the library."

"Guilty," I pleaded. "I was desperate for attention."

"Well, now you're in the spotlight you've always coveted. So I have to give you more advice, I'm afraid. Be wary of too much attention. Be wary of the critics. Don't expect the whole world to open its arms to you."

"All my notices have been good so far."

"You're in your honeymoon phase, Lang Lang."

"I understand," I said, but I disagreed with Mr. Graffman. Naively, I thought the critics would always love me. Rather than gloating about my successes, I should have remembered my second piano competition back in Shenyang, which I entered expecting to take home first prize. I had won my first competition; why wouldn't I ace the second? Instead, I had come home with a stuffed yellow dog.

As usual, my father was more confident than I was. As my agent began to call regularly—as though suddenly we were best friends—he relayed offers from different orchestras, as well as from recording companies such as Deutsche Grammophon and Telarc. Famous people I didn't know were phoning or e-mailing to congratulate me on Ravinia. It was hard to keep my feet on the ground.

I did a live performance recording at Tanglewood, another famous outdoor festival, near Lenox, Massachusetts. That engagement was followed by my long-anticipated debut at Carnegie Hall, where I played with the Baltimore Symphony under Yuri Temirkanov—another dream come true. Then came my European debut with the St. Petersburg Philharmonic, and a London stop at the Proms, to play Rachmaninoff's Third Piano Concerto.

My father still accompanied me to almost every performance, as if he were my chaperone or my shadow. I had mixed emotions about his company, because while I was grateful for his years of loyalty and persistence, I had earned my wings and thought I was capable of soloing now.

A whirlwind schedule of eighty performances a year left me little free time. Making friends was out of the question because I never stayed in one city very long. Even my piano lessons with Mr. Graffman had to be done over the phone. It was run, run, and run some more. Frequent flyer miles became as familiar to me as airport food courts.

On the positive side, I was delighted finally to be making good money, and my first major purchase was a house in downtown Philadelphia. In the rap world I would call it my "crib." My friends thought I was crazy because I was on the road more than I was at home, so why not just rent somewhere? But whenever I remembered my childhood of poverty and uncertainty, I felt it was essential to have an anchor, a place to call my own.

My father settled into his own room on the second floor and I insisted my mother fly over from China. I badly wanted to keep my promise to bring us all together. I invited my mom to visit for a month, but half that time I was on tour. She didn't mind. After all, it was like a dream that the three of us had a house in America.

"Is your success everything you thought it would be, Lang Lang?" she asked one day.

"It's overwhelming," I admitted. "For years I couldn't wait for things to speed up. Now I want them to slow down, just a little."

I told her about adjusting to a dizzying travel schedule and hanging out with my friends. My emotions were scattered. I was even feeling homesick for Shenyang, my old friends and teachers. The New York Philharmonic was scheduling an Asian tour in a few months with stops in Beijing and Shanghai. I told my mother I hoped to be a part of it.

"I'll make sure all your friends from Shenyang come," she promised.

"That would be incredible," I said, giving her a hug.

Then I learned that, in a matter of only weeks, the Philadelphia Orchestra, under Maestro Wolfgang Sawallisch, would be organizing its own tour of China, and wanted me to play a grand concert in Beijing's Great Hall of the People. The president of China would be attending. The whole country would be watching on television. My heart swelled in anticipation. I would be returning in triumph to the country of my birth. And I'd be returning with the same orchestra that had accompanied President Nixon on his historic 1972 trip to Beijing, where he had expanded political and trading relations between the two countries.

The concert organizers in China didn't want me to play at all because they wanted an international star.

"We need a major star when Philadelphia plays in the Great Hall of the People," the presenter told Maestro Sawallisch. "Lang Lang is hardly an international celebrity. In China, he has been all but forgotten."

Philadelphia was surprised to hear this, as was New York, but no one was more shocked or heartbroken than I was.

When I conferred with Maestro Sawallisch, he told me not to worry. He'd call his friends in Beijing and straighten everything out. A few days later, my chances still looked bleak. "China's organizers are not budging," the maestro told me on the phone. "They want the winner of the most recent International Tchaikovsky Competition to play."

"What did you say?"

"I defended you. I wouldn't accept a substitute. I said, 'Lang Lang has to play with us because he's a son of Philadelphia—a proud student of Curtis—as well as China. If Lang Lang can't play with us, Philadelphia's not coming to Beijing.' "

"Wow." I was stunned, and grateful for the support. "How did he respond?"

"Silence at first. He finally said he'd talk to his superiors and get back to me."

The next few days brought mixed messages. At first the concert was definitely on, then it was definitely off. In the background was lots of political noise having little to do with me. A U.S. spy plane had been accused of entering Chinese airspace and had collided with a Chinese fighter jet. Suddenly I was worried that the Philadelphia Orchestra couldn't even go because of the political tension.

Another week passed. Very fortunately, my agent received a call from the U.S. State Department: Philadelphia and I would be welcome to play at the Great Hall of the People! I was incredibly relieved, and once again I fantasized about my homecoming.

{ 23 }

It was June 2001 when I set foot on Chinese soil, with my mother at my side. I had barely stepped off the plane when I was bombarded with reporters' questions. What had I been doing since I left China? Why hadn't I been in touch with anyone in Beijing? Was I hiding from something? I quickly realized that no one had heard about me substituting for André Watts at Ravinia, or my subsequent leap to fame. Apparently, what made news in America didn't always spill over to Asia.

I took several minutes to explain everything that had happened in my four years away. I expected a few smiles, at least a nod or two of recognition, but the reporters' faces remained bloodless and their tone unchanged.

"What contests have you won?" someone shouted.

"In America, contests aren't important," I replied. "After a certain point, you aren't expected to compete."

"If you haven't won any awards," said another writer, "why did Philadelphia choose you?"

"I guess because they liked me."

No one laughed. Everybody wanted to know why I hadn't entered any competitions. They were suspicious. Was I afraid of losing? Was I still sharp enough to compete with other young talent coming out of China?

I had forgotten how insanely competitive my home-land was. After the brutal press conference, my mother tried to console me.

"Darling," she said, "they will all change their minds once they hear you play."

On the phone, my father was incensed when I told him about the press conference. "If I were there, I'd tell them all to go to hell."

I was glad he had stayed home.

Maestro Sawallisch couldn't have been more support-ive of me or the position of the orchestra, but that meant nothing to the local media. It was me, not the maestro, whom everybody followed around unhappily, as if I had abandoned my country for another. I felt as if they wanted me to fail at the Great Hall of the People.

Perhaps I should have been rattled or intimidated when I sat down to play the following afternoon. But I wasn't. No matter who was watching or what they were thinking, I was tired of arguing and justifying my existence. None of that mattered. I just wanted to be myself and play. I drew strength from knowing my mother and friends and teachers from Shenyang were in the audience, that they loved me and cared about me as much as I did about them.

Honoring my agreement, I played a Mendelssohn concerto. Mendelssohn is not Tchaikovsky or Beethoven. His compositions are lyrical and sensitive, not overly intense or dramatic or filled with technical difficulty, all of which Chinese music critics traditionally like. I knew that most of the audience wanted to hear something difficult that would justify my lack of prizes the last four years. They wanted to be bowled over.

When I finished and took a bow, I was received with warmth and affection, but not the thunderous ovations I'd gotten used to in America. (A year later, though, everything changed; I was a huge success after playing a Rachmaninoff piano concerto.) After Beijing, Maestro Sawallisch and the Philadelphia Orchestra continued on their China tour, but as previously arranged, I flew back to the United States, and was happy to do so. The only difficult thing was leaving my mother. I hugged her fiercely at the airport and promised we would be together again soon.

As the plane crossed the Pacific, my head started to ache and nausea swept over me. I could barely make it through customs in Philadelphia. My father rushed me home, where I slept for a week, chilled and feverish. I had just begun to recover when a familiar figure hovered over me with the purposeful, urgent gaze I had come to know well. My father didn't want to talk about my disappointment in China. That was history. He wanted to remind me of my numerous upcoming commitments, and that I hadn't practiced in ten days.

One of the commitments was to play Rachmaninoff with Maestro Eschenbach and the Chicago Symphony Orchestra at Ravinia, which would always have a special place in my heart. The good fortune of having the chance to replace André Watts had been my gift from the musical gods, and it was my obligation to continue my musical career. I was the new golden boy of classical piano, and I couldn't let anyone down. But in my heart it wasn't just an obligation. It would be sheer joy to return.

I played at Ravinia to large and enthusiastic crowds. Many who had seen me the first time returned and brought their friends. But just when I felt reassured of my rising star, something emerged from the darkness to try to extinguish my light.

For the last two years, since my debut at Ravinia, I had received nothing but affection and well-wishing from critics, fans, and musicians. The golden boy could do no wrong. This was my "honeymoon period," as Mr. Graffman liked to refer to it, an idea that I stubbornly denied. I thought my career would be different from all others. I thought I would be on a pedestal forever.

But with my third appearance at Ravinia, while the maestro and I thought I'd played superbly, a very influential critic disagreed. He reminded me of Professor Angry, only worse. He didn't keep his feelings to himself or whisper them to just a few people. He wrote openly in the media. This was so different from his original review, in which he'd called me the "biggest talent in years." This time I was at Ravinia in residency for five days, during which time I played five different programs, including a solo piano recital, a four-hands recital with Christoph Eschenbach, a Grieg piano concerto, Rachmaninoff's Rhapsody on a Theme of Paganini, and a duet recital with my father on the erhu. This was the first time I'd played with my father in America. As if my piano were a lethal weapon, this critic said, I was murdering classical music. I had committed a crime against Grieg and Rachmaninoff. He wrote not one but two attacks, as he had plenty of venom to spare. He hated not just me but Mr. Eschenbach for being my patron and co-conspirator and for shamelessly supporting a crazy pianist. My career should be given an early death, he implied, because the world of classical music would be better off if no one heard from me again.

Maestro was furious and wanted to sue the writer and the newspaper for libel. He wanted a public apology. At first I was calm, but gradually disbelief crept over me. Why did this critic think he knew more about interpreting Grieg and Rachmaninoff than I did? All pianists treated the great works differently. That's what made my world so fascinating—it was all about style, interpretation, structure, and nuance. Tchaikovsky wasn't around to tell anyone how to play his music. Instructions hadn't been left in his will. His compositions had longevity because in fact there were multiple ways to translate them. Music wasn't science; it was poetry, romance, and spirituality.

But my opinion didn't matter. One critic infected another and then another, and soon I was labeled egotistical and lacking in sensitivity. I was accused of "Lang Lang–izing" everything my fingers touched. I was too personal, too subjective, too self-indulgent, and too Romantic, if not outright schmaltzy. Mr. Graffman told me to be calm and take the long perspective. Careers weren't determined by critics, he advised, they were determined by the artist—his perseverance, his self-confidence, and being true to his talent.

In addition to testing my resolve, the critics' attacks had a silver lining. My sudden controversy increased the number of my bookings and my fees. I learned that classical music fans had strong opinions, and the more detractors I had, the more my supporters rushed to my defense and wanted to hear me in concert. Those who'd never heard me came to make up their own minds.

To my surprise, my father during this period was less than supportive. We argued frequently about the importance of critics. I said most were fools, but he insisted that even fools should be listened to. When the media in Beijing had attacked me, I pointed out, he had come to my defense, but now he was distancing himself. Taking the critics' side reminded me of the way he had once backed Professor Angry, believing her even when I told him she was lying. I was the boy whom he'd loved and whose talent he'd nurtured from birth; where were his fatherly love and loyalty now? What kind of father was he? I tried to understand. Maybe it was all about control, keeping me off balance—I never knew whose side he would take next—but that explanation hardly brought me comfort.

While I continued touring and making money, behind my confident exterior cracks were beginning to appear. I had periods of depression and self-doubt. I had always been superstitious, to the point of being slightly neurotic, but now I was worrying incessantly about my health, particularly injuries to my arms and hands. I became obsessed with the possibility of hurting myself and not being able to play again. If I couldn't play, I thought, I'd go mad. If I went mad, I'd have no reason to live.

If you fear something too much, sometimes it comes true. If you're driving a car, for example, and you're constantly afraid of running into a tree, one day perhaps it's inevitable that you'll drive right into one. It wasn't quite that way with me, but close. I had been practicing in Philadelphia on a friend's piano, one that Horowitz had used, and because the ivory was worn and thin, I pressed too hard on the keys. Suddenly, a bolt of pain spiraled through my pinky and up my arm. The jolt was so sudden and sharp that I stopped playing immediately.

My father—the good, supportive one—rushed me to a doctor, who suspected that I had a minor injury and forbade me to play for a month. If I risked practicing, he warned, the tendonitis would only worsen. I was just like an athlete sidelined with an injury, like Michael Jordan or Allen Iverson—I felt frustrated and helpless and couldn't wait to return to the game. It happened to everyone, I had to accept that. But my injury depressed and worried me. If I didn't play for a month, how much would my skills deteriorate? Would I simply go crazy from boredom? For someone who couldn't be patient under the best of circumstances, this new crisis would really test me.

The first days of staying away from the piano were excruciating. It was like having a terrible, insatiable itch and knowing you couldn't scratch it. Concerts were cancelled and schedules juggled, but no one could be sure when I would be totally healthy to play. I hated uncertainty. I began to worry again about my career. What if the tendonitis never totally healed? What kind of pianist would I be?

For help I called Dick Doran, my cultural mentor, who came over right away with books on World War Two and the Shakespeare plays we hadn't had time to cover.

"This is a blessing," he declared.

"What?"

"Being incapacitated," he said cheerily.

"Why?"

"You love reading about World War Two. I know that. There are hundreds of books on the subject. Let's start with these," he said, handing me a pile. "And our beloved Shakespeare! We can't ignore the Bard. You never have time to read on the road, do you?"

"Very little," I admitted.

"Like I said, a blessing."

Dick had a point. We talked about achieving balance in my life. Music alone, no matter how talented I was, made me a lopsided person, he said. I needed to be well rounded. I needed depth. Depth would make me a better musician and a better human being.

I began reading voraciously, and when I tired of books for the moment, I invited my friends to my house, telling them I had made a resolution, even though it wasn't quite New Year's. I was going to practice leading a normal life, a balanced life. At least for one month, I wasn't going to think about Liszt or Beethoven or Rimsky-Korsakov. I was going to read the newspaper every day, study World War Two and the Bard, watch movies, and take long walks for exercise. My friends were skeptical. The only thing I knew, they said, was the piano. I had as much chance at leading a normal life as the proverbial cow had of jumping over the moon.

I was determined to prove them wrong. I began watching James Bond movies, studied Picasso and the Impressionists at the Philadelphia Museum of Art, and listened to Gershwin at home, loving the colors in his music as much as I did the fall leaves. Every time I got antsy, I closed my eyes and took deep breaths.

My month-long sabbatical turned out to be one of the best things to happen in a long time. While the piano is a beautiful thing, I also learned that so are friendship, Shakespeare, Eminem, a slam dunk, a chocolate sundae, Frank Sinatra, and girls. The universe is as deep, varied, and mysterious as the places you are willing to explore.

When the month was over, the doctor pronounced my hand and arm healthy. I would return to my piano, I knew, with a healthier mind and spirit, ready to take on the world with a fresh perspective. Life would no longer be solely about conquering and winning. It would also be about negotiating the often invisible line between passion and moderation, heart and intellect, rigid discipline and letting go.

{ 24 }

A few years have passed since my injury, but the lesson of balance has stayed with me. Teachers such as Gary Graffman and Dick Doran put me on that path, and my great new teacher, Maestro Daniel Barenboim, kept me on it. I met Mr. Barenboim after I'd played with the New York Philharmonic at Lincoln Center before the Asia tour. Zarin Mehta, the director of the New York Philharmonic, knocked on my dressing room door.

"Lang Lang," he said, "I'd like you to meet someone very special. He watched you perform tonight and wanted to say hello. This is Daniel Barenboim."

I was tired from my performance but came awake when I gazed at my unanticipated visitor. No introduction to Maestro Barenboim was necessary. I had seen enough photos and read so many articles on the world-famous conductor and pianist that I would have recognized the white-haired gentleman anywhere.

"How do you do?" I said. "This is a great honor."

The next words that came out of my mouth embarrassed me—they were so childlike—but they were genuine nonetheless. "Oh, Maestro, will you teach me?"

"Why, of course," he said, his words as natural as my own request had felt awkward. "But please call me Daniel."

I suddenly thought of an expression I had learned long ago in China: "When the student is ready, the teacher appears." I gave Daniel a hug, and so began a friendship that has never wavered.

Born in Buenos Aires of Jewish parents, Daniel eventually became a citizen of Israel and Spain as well as Argentina. He is an acknowledged genius not just in music but in his creative efforts to ease political and ethnic tensions in the world. As his musical career soared, he was named the music director of the Chicago Symphony Orchestra and of the Deutsche Staatsoper in Berlin. For a devout Jew to lead Germany's most prominent orchestra was compelling evidence that the past—World War Two and the concentration camps—could be healed. When he started his own orchestra for young Arab and Israeli musicians, bringing understanding between Palestinians and Jews, he showed that music is also the universal language of peace for the future. Music, like sports, is at its heart not about competition or taking sides or ideology, but about harmony, respect, and the expression of the individual.

Daniel Barenboim, with his multiple citizenships and ability to speak eight languages, is the perfect illustration of how music could transcend cultural barriers. As terms go, East and West represent convenient geopolitical and cultural boundaries, but to any serious artist—painters, musicians, dancers, or writers—they are meant to be crossed. And in crossing them, both the artist and his audience are enriched.

After my piano lessons, Daniel and I often talked about the interconnectedness of classical music. German music was different from French, Finnish from Russian, Chinese from Spanish, and so on. But for all those differences, an exceptional musician from one country or culture could master the music of another. Critics said that I had a Russian soul because I was naturally drawn to the technical difficulties that Tchaikovsky and Rachmaninoff infused into their music, not to mention the often bombastic drama. Even though I was Chinese, I had somehow learned to speak the language of the Russian composers.

Daniel and I also discussed the interplay between emotion and intellect in music. For many composers, such as Beethoven, emotion ruled. Yet Beethoven didn't allow himself to be simply swept away by his feelings. He needed intellectual discipline to structure that emotion; otherwise his works would have lacked the power they ultimately convey. I knew this was an area in which I still needed work. With time, Daniel said, I too would acquire that balance between emotion and intellect. His mentor was Arthur Rubinstein, and from that I have reflected on my life and how to balance it. My two biggest heroes are Horowitz and Rubinstein, and now I feel even more connected to them because I have the honor of working with Gary Graffman and Daniel Barenboim, who were directly associated with these celebrated Russian superstars.

In 2004, a very nice lady who worked at the United Nations, and who had seen my enthusiasm with children, introduced me to the executive director of the United Nations Children's Fund (UNICEF). A few months later, I was greatly honored to be appointed international goodwill ambassador to UNICEF, the youngest in its history. In that capacity, I would travel to different parts of the world and see the devastating effects that AIDS and other diseases had on children.

I immediately informed UNICEF that I would leave at the first break in my touring schedule. My decision was based on my love for children, on a desire to continue to balance and deepen my life, and on memories of my own impoverished childhood, which I knew was nothing compared to what I would discover in Africa.

I flew from New York to Dar es Salaam, the capital of Tanzania. After resting for a day, I toured the sprawling city, witnessing the deep pockets of poverty as well as some incredible architecture and mosques. Dar es

Salaam, which literally means "abode of peace," was a city of striking contrasts—squalor and beauty, its economy struggling yet with money for development rushing in from countries such as China, a climate of political repression and favoritism but with growing opportunities for change. This port city of two and a half million people was small by Chinese standards, but so complex in its racial and ethnic diversity that I was fascinated by everything I learned.

Later, a Jeep bearing a UNICEF flag met me and took me to numerous villages, schools, and hospitals outside of Dar es Salaam. I also visited indigenous peoples such as the Maasai, a tall and colorfully dressed people with expressive faces and a musical culture of wild and graceful dancing. They won my heart. I thought of the rap world I knew in Philadelphia. The Maasai were another precious subculture that I prayed wouldn't be lost to assimilation or neglect or poverty.

At some schools where I stopped, the children would entertain me with their stories or plays about AIDS, and I saw firsthand many who were dying from this plague. Where I could, I played the piano for them and watched their faces break into smiles, even laughter. I met teachers, doctors, and volunteers from dozens of countries. I thanked them individually for saving and building lives and communities. As a UNICEF ambassador, I promised to spread the word at my concerts and in interviews that even more help was needed here and needed quickly.

Many times I found myself reduced to tears at the

appalling conditions. Yet by the end of my trip, heartened by my mission to bring world awareness to the plight of these children, my tears were ones of hope and determination. I had always been blessed with a strong will and the discipline to succeed, and this task would be no different.

Similar to my universe of classical music, all of us live in an increasingly interrelated, interdependent world. I believe East and West will coexist best when each admits it needs to learn from the other. No one side is superior. We're all each other's teachers and each other's students—Muslims and Christians, Jews and Arabs, First World and Third.

As I've grown up, the loneliness of my days in Shenyang and Beijing have been replaced by an awareness that no one is truly alone. Quoting the English poet John Donne: "No man is an island." To survive, we must all be connected by the bridge of responsibility and compassion.

A few weeks after my trip to Tanzania, I was back in China, wandering the streets of old Beijing. A boy suddenly approached me with a broad smile. He knew who I was and introduced himself. "Hey, Lang Lang," he said, "I know that you're on Deutsche Grammophon. I see that Mozart has a deal on that label as well."

I smiled to myself. He really didn't know that Mozart was long gone. But as I kept walking, I thought about that boy and reached a different conclusion. Mozart was alive and well, and so was classical music in China. Sales of pianos were falling in the United States for the time being, but they were rising sharply in China. The human need for music was about a quest for immortality, about the timelessness of mystery and magic. As long as there was one man or woman left on earth, I thought, there would have to be music.

Over the years I have learned that being number one is not the only goal a person should have. There is no denying that I am extremely proud of all I have achieved through diligence and discipline and hard work. My family and I have made great sacrifices. The only thing that always sustained me throughout all of the difficult years was my passion for music and my love for playing the piano. Making music is like breathing for me. I cannot fathom my life without music.

As I look ahead I know that my goals include helping young people discover the power of music—the joy of making or listening to it. I have started a foundation, the Lang Lang International Music Foundation. My foundation will support education for musical training, and it will provide scholarships for young people from all corners of the world. I want to inspire young people to learn about the great composers and hear sounds they have never heard before. Classical music is just as cool as the music kids love today. I want kids to know this. It is so true! The composers who created new sounds centuries ago were the rock stars of their time. They were daring and innovative, and my hope is that young people today will not only listen to these sensational composers and appreciate sounds they have not heard before but also be inspired to re-create these wonderful works and compose music of their own. As my own fingers fly over the keyboard, I hope that the music I play opens up doors and minds. This is as important to me as being number one.

LANG LANG'S VITAL STATISTICS AND SOME OF HIS FAVORITE THINGS

NICKNAME: Liang Liang

BIRTH DATE: June 14, 1982

BIRTHPLACE: Shenyang, China

HEIGHT: 5' 10"

WEIGHT: 162 pounds

HAIR COLOR: Black

EYE COLOR: Brown

PARENTS' NAMES: Lang Guoren (father), Zhou Xiulan (mother)

FAVORITE BOOK (IN ENGLISH): *Hamlet*

FAVORITE BOOK (IN CHINESE): *The Monkey King*

FAVORITE SPORTS: Basketball, soccer, Ping-Pong

FAVORITE MUSICIANS (CLASSICAL AND CONTEMPORARY): Vladimir Horowitz, Arthur Rubinstein, Luciano

Pavarotti, Plácido Domingo, Andrea Bocelli, David Foster (songwriter/producer), Tan Dun (composer), Christina Aguilera, Beyoncé, Alicia Keys

FAVORITE ACTORS: Brad Pitt, Johnny Depp, Tom Cruise, George Clooney, Jackie Chan

FAVORITE ACTRESSES: Sarah Jessica Parker, Naomi Watts, Angelina Jolie, Jennifer Lopez, Zhang Ziyi, Gong Li

FAVORITE MOVIES: *Crouching Tiger, Hidden Dragon; Spider-Man 3; The Godfather; The Matrix*

FAVORITE TV SHOWS: *Sex and the City, The Simpsons, The X-Files*

FAVORITE VACATION SPOTS: Sicily, Italy; Lucerne, Switzerland; Miami Beach, Florida; Hainan Island, China; Rio de Janeiro, Brazil

FAVORITE FOODS: Mom's homemade dumplings, Japanese sushi, Korean BBQ, Italian pasta

FAVORITE DRINKS: Water, orange juice, milk

FAVORITE COLORS: Blue, red, black

FAVORITE CHILDHOOD MEMORY: Listening to my mother's stories, going to catch dragonflies with a childhood friend

FAVORITE CITY: New York City

HABITS: Massaging fingers, rubbing chin when stressed

BEST SUBJECTS IN SCHOOL: Literature, history, geography

WORST SUBJECTS IN SCHOOL: Math, science

LANGUAGES SPOKEN: Chinese, English; can say "thank you" in twenty languages

BEST QUALITY: Honesty

WORST QUALITY: Impatience

LITTLE-KNOWN FACT: When Lang Lang's plane lands, he always switches on the overhead light and counts to ten, then turns it off, to bring luck to the place he's about to visit

BEST BIRTHDAY GIFT RECEIVED: An original handwritten letter from Liszt to his best student, given by a friend

HOBBIES: Shopping for clothes; learning about high technology; using high-tech gadgets

BEST WAY TO RELAX: Chinese massage (body and foot), lying on the beach, walking in the forest, watching a comedy show on TV, listening to a Mozart opera

TIPS FOR A FAN: Eat lots of fruit, be a natural listener

PROFESSIONAL AMBITION: Make classical music known to all young children around the world, make classical music cool

GLOSSARY OF WESTERN COMPOSERS WITH LANG LANG'S COMMENTARY

There is so much to say about so many important composers, but I have selected a few I have grown up playing, and added some short remarks.

WOLFGANG AMADEUS MOZART: For me, Mozart is the most gifted musical genius. He is like Monkey King to me—so very important. Mozart's music changes characters, so you can envision a flower—or a girl—or a grandfather! Your imagination is always inspired.

LUDWIG VAN BEETHOVEN: Many people already know that Beethoven had a hot temperament. What I like about his music is the enormous intensity and power of the sound.

FRÉDÉRIC CHOPIN: Listening to or playing Chopin, one hears the most beautiful, poetic melodies. He is absolutely the incarnation of Romantic music.

FRANZ LISZT: The opposite of Chopin would be Liszt. Whether you have ever liked classical music or not, when you hear the music of Liszt you get crazy. In fact, I'd say he's a mega–rock star—then and now.

SERGEI RACHMANINOFF: This musician's works are even more Romantic than the music of Chopin. Even those people who say they do not like classical music usually like his music.

CLAUDE DEBUSSY: This man was the first composer to connect me to the great paintings of the Impressionists. Everything he wrote is like a fairy tale.

GEORGE GERSHWIN: For me this American composer, inspired by the jazz world, really created what seems to be the school of American music.

ROBERT SCHUMANN: The music of this composer is complex—at times there are beautiful passages, and then there are passages that make you feel like your heart is breaking. A unique experience.

JOHANN SEBASTIAN BACH: For me, Bach's music is the closest to God. In his music a listener hears so many different voices. I'd say his music is the most spiritual of all.

PYOTR ILLICH TCHAIKOVSKY: This is music that feels noble. This composer created music with huge phrases and a big heart.

JOHANN STRAUSS THE ELDER, JOHANN STRAUSS THE YOUNGER: Both father and son created music for dance that is always associated by me, and so many others, with the New Year. What would a year be without the waltz?

Of course there are many other composers to discuss. I hope that readers will listen to the music of these great composers and find out more about each one.

ACKNOWLEDGMENTS

Thank you to David Ritz, Michael French, Jean Jacques Cesbron, Nora Benary, Beverly Horowitz, and the entire Random House Children's Books team. I would also like to thank my family members, friends, mentors, teachers, fellow artists, and all of the people who have supported me.

LANG LANG

Celebrated in the musical capitals of the world, Lang Lang has demonstrated an extraordinary level of musicianship over the widest of repertoires. Born in 1982 in Shenyang, China, he began piano lessons at the age of three. At the age of five, he won the Shenyang Piano Competition and gave his first public recital. He has performed solo recitals and concerts with major orchestras all over the world. Lang Lang is the first Chinese pianist to be engaged by the Berlin Philharmonic, the Vienna Philharmonic, and all the leading American orchestras. Although he is on tour most of the year, he has homes in New York City and Beijing.

MICHAEL FRENCH

Michael French has published twenty books, including fiction for adults and young adults, biographies, and art criticism. He has adapted many acclaimed works for young people. This adaptation is based on Lang Lang's autobiography, written with David Ritz. Michael French divides his time between Santa Barbara, California, and Santa Fe, New Mexico.